VITTORIA 1813

VITTORIA 1813

WRITTEN BY
IAN FLETCHER

BATTLESCENE ARTWORK BY
BILL YOUNGHUSBAND

First publshed in Great Britain in 1998 by Osprey Publishing
Elms Court, Chapel Way Botley, Oxford OX2 9LP United Kingdom
Email: info@ospreypublishing.com

Also published as Campaign 59 *Vittoria 1813*

ISBN 1 84176 151 6

Editors: Ian MacGregor and Marcus Cowper
Design: Luise Roberts

Colour bird's eye view illustrations by Trevor Lawrence
Wargaming Vittoria by Arthur Harman
Cartography by Micromap
Battlescene artwork by Bill Younghusband
Origination by Anglia Graphics Ltd.
Printed in China through World Print Ltd.

00 01 02 03 04   10 9 8 7 6 5 4 3 2 1

FOR CATALOGUE OF ALL BOOKS PUBLISHED BY OSPREY MILITARY AND AVIATION
PLEASE WRITE TO:

The Marketing Manager, Osprey Direct UK, PO Box 140,
Wellingborough, Northants, NN8 4ZA, United Kingdom
Email: info@ospreydirect.co.uk

The Marketing Manager, Osprey Direct USA, PO Box 130, Sterling
Heights, MI 48311-0130, United States of America
Email: info@ospreydirectusa.com

Visit Osprey at:
www.ospreypublishing.com

KEY TO MILITARY SERIES SYMBOLS

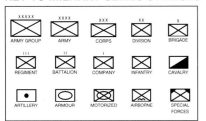

xxxxx	xxxx	xxx	xx	x
ARMY GROUP	ARMY	CORPS	DIVISION	BRIGADE
lll	ll	l		
REGIMENT	BATTALION	COMPANY	INFANTRY	CAVALRY
ARTILLERY	ARMOUR	MOTORIZED	AIRBORNE	SPECIAL FORCES

Acknowledgements

No book on any campaign in history can really be done effectively
without a visit to the actual field of battle. I followed the whole
campaign trail from Salamanca to Vittoria in the company of my
good friends Dave Chantler, Hugh Macdonald-Buchanan, Richard
Old and John Seabrook, who, as usual, were of great assistance in
plotting the various movements and in working out dispositions at
some of the more obscure places along the way – San Millan,
Osma and Morales de Toro in particular. Thanks chaps.

FRONT COVER: Wellington and his staff at the battle of Vittoria
(courtesy of Ian Fletcher)

BACK COVER: British Hussars smash into the French rearguard towards
the end of the battle of Vittoria (courtesy of Ian Fletcher)

PAGE 2 **The 71st Highlanders in action on the heights of
Puebla. The battalion lost its commanding officer, Cadogan,
during the battle. He was mortally wounded but insisted on
being propped up on a couple of knapsacks in order to be
able to watch his men's progress. After a painting by
Wollen.**

CONTENTS

THE WAR IN THE PENINSULA 7

THE VITTORIA CAMPAIGN 16

THE OPPOSING COMMANDERS 25
Wellington • The French

ORDER OF BATTLE 30

THE BATTLE OF VITTORIA 34
The Battlefield • French Dispositions
Allied Dispositions • The Battle Begins • The Decisive Blow
The French Retreat • The Pursuit Stalls

AFTERMATH 74

THE BATTLEFIELD TODAY 80

WARGAMING VITTORIA 88
Introduction • The Battle of Vittoria

FURTHER READING 94

INDEX 95

THE WAR IN THE PENINSULA

On 1 August 1808 Sir Arthur Wellesley, later to become 1st Duke of Wellington, landed at Figueira de Foz in Portugal at the head of 9,000 British soldiers. It was the first act in a long, hard war which would see the British army, in company with its Portuguese and Spanish allies, march back and forth across the Iberian peninsula until it eventually crossed the Bidassoa river on 7 October 1813 to begin the invasion of France; the war ended in triumph in April 1814. The landing in 1808 was not the first act of the Peninsular War, however, because on 18 October 1807 General Andoche Junot had set off from the Pyrenees and across Spain with 25,000 French troops on a long, gruelling march to the Portuguese capital, Lisbon. He had been despatched there by Napoleon Bonaparte, in order to seize the Portuguese regent, John, who had refused to bow to French pressure and impose the so-called 'Continental Blockade'. The latter was supposed to ensure that all European ports were closed to British trade, and was an attempt to starve Britain into submission. Junot arrived on

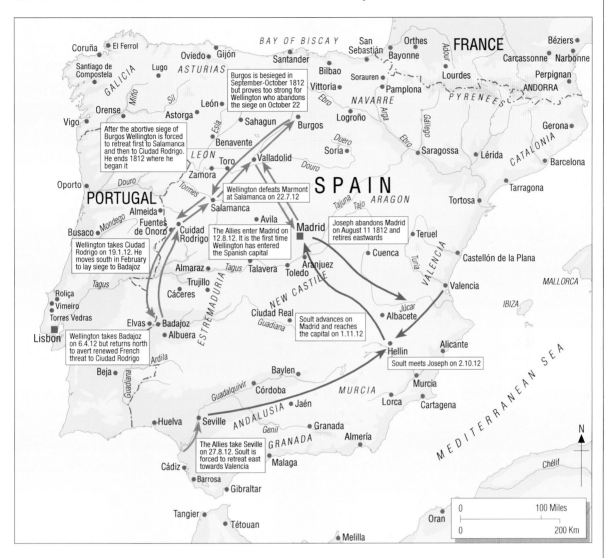

Burgos is besieged in September-October 1812 but proves too strong for Wellington who abandons the siege on October 22

After the abortive siege of Burgos Wellington is forced to retreat first to Salamanca and then to Ciudad Rodrigo. He ends 1812 where he began it

Wellington defeats Marmont at Salamanca on 22.7.12

Joseph abandons Madrid on August 11 1812 and retires eastwards

The Allies enter Madrid on 12.8.12. It is the first time Wellington has entered the Spanish capital

Wellington takes Ciudad Rodrigo on 19.1.12. He moves south in February to lay siege to Badajoz

Wellington takes Badajoz on 6.4.12 but returns north to avert renewed French threat to Ciudad Rodrigo

Soult advances on Madrid and reaches the capital on 1.11.12

Soult meets Joseph on 2.10.12

The Allies take Seville on 27.8.12. Soult is forced to retreat east towards Valencia

30 November and found to his dismay that the Portuguese royal family had sailed to safety in Brazil the day before. However, he could console himself with the thought that he had placed Portugal under the yoke of Napoleon's France.

The subsequent months saw a feud erupt within the Spanish royal family, notably between Ferdinand VII and his father, King Carlos IV. This feud had been simmering away for some time before the hapless pair were summoned to Bayonne by Napoleon, whose help both men had sought. However, Napoleon simply declared his intention to dissolve the Bourbon family and install a French prince on the Spanish throne. All Spain was outraged, and insurrections took place all over the country; in the Asturias the population turned on French troops who over the previous months had been busy installing themselves in Spanish towns and fortresses, pretending to prepare to support Junot in Portugal.

The most famous Spanish revolt – the 'Dos de Mayo' – took place on 2 May 1808, when the Madrid mob turned against the French garrison in the Spanish capital. The rising was ruthlessly suppressed by the French commander Murat. Napoleon's brother, Joseph, travelled to Spain in the wake of the risings to assume the title of King of Spain. Ironically, Joseph is considered to have been a fair ruler and was viewed with a good degree of sympathy even by the Spaniards themselves. He entered Madrid on 20 July 1808 and ruled until his crushing defeat at Vittoria.

The damage to French prestige had been done, however, and representatives from the Asturias and other insurgent juntas travelled to London to seek assistance from Britain, their former enemy. The Spaniards arrived in London on 7 June 1808 and spent a long, hard five weeks trying to convince the British government that theirs was a cause worth fighting. If the British government needed any further coaxing, it came with the news that on 14 July a French army under Dupont had surrendered at Baylen to the Spanish army of General Castanos. The British government decided, therefore, to send a force to Portugal. The 9,000 troops, who ironically had originally been earmarked for an operation against the Spanish colonies in South America, were diverted to Portugal under Wellesley.

Sir Arthur Wellesley was joined in Portugal by Sir Brent Spencer with a further 5,000 troops, and on 17 August 1808 Wellesley fought his first battle, between the small villages of Rolica and Columbeira. His victory was followed four days later by a more notable one, when he soundly defeated a French army under Junot at Vimeiro, just a few miles to the south. The victory trapped Junot and his army against the Lisbon peninsula with no way out. Junot had little choice but to sue for an armistice, and the result was the infamous Convention of Cintra, drawn up between Junot and Kellerman on the French side, and Wellesley, Dalrymple and Burrard – the latter two generals having arrived in Portugal to supersede Wellesley – on the other. The Convention of Cintra allowed the defeated French troops to sail back to France with all their accumulated arms and plunder. This was bad enough, but the fact that they were transported in the ships of the Royal Navy made the convention all too unpalatable for the British public, and all three generals were recalled to Britain to face a court of inquiry.

In the meantime the British army was placed under the command of Sir John Moore. In October 1808 Moore embarked upon his ill-fated

LEFT **The battlefield of Morales de Toro. The 10th, 15th and 18th Hussars broke and pursued the 26th Dragoons across this plain before being halted at the foot of the heights upon which were positioned French infantry, cavalry and artillery. This picture was taken from the heights. Morales is on the skyline in the far distance while the river Bayas is marked by the tree line in the centre.**

LEFT **The 42nd Highlanders in action in the village of Elvina during the battle of Corunna, 16 January 1809. The battle allowed Sir John Moore's army to get away but it cost him his own life.**

BELOW **The bridge over the Douro at Toro. It was crossed by Hill's infantry on 3 June, the artillery and baggage using a ford close by. Although the French had blown the bridge earlier, only one arch was destroyed. Lieutenant Pringle, of the Royal Engineers, managed to get everybody across by means of some ladders which were laid at each end of the gap with long planks of wood between the lower rungs. The infantry crossed in single file, taking Hill's four divisions all of 3 June and the morning of 4 June to cross.**

RIGHT **The bridge at Puente Arenas over the Ebro, crossed by Hill's column during the advance to Vittoria, thus outflanking yet another major French defensive position.**

Corunna campaign, a brave attempt to buy time for the disorganised Spanish armies but one which cost him his life, at the battle of Corunna on 16 January 1809. Three months later Wellesley was back in Portugal, and on 12 May 1809, in one of the most daring operations of the war, his men crossed the Douro at Oporto to expel the French under Marshal Soult from Portugal. Thus Wellesley had brought the second French invasion of Portugal to an abrupt end, just as he had the first the previous year.

Soon afterwards Wellesley moved south to link up with the ageing Spanish general Cuesta. The two men were to march against the out-numbered French force under Marshal Victor, but as Moore had discovered the previous year, any combined operation with the Spaniards was fraught with difficulty; while Wellesley and his men limbered up to march against the French, they found Cuesta still in bed, and a fine opportunity was lost. By the time the two armies had sorted themselves out, Victor had received reinforcements from Sebastiani and an Allied retreat was called for. On 27 and 28 July the two sides clashed at Talavera, a hard-fought battle which resulted in a victory for the Allies. It was also a success which earned Wellesley elevation to the peerage: on 16 September 1809 he duly signed himself 'Wellington'.

There was to be an interval of some 14 months between Talavera and Wellington's next battle – at Busaco on 27 September 1810. Meanwhile, the two border fortresses of Ciudad Rodrigo and Almeida had fallen to the French, and the expected invasion was underway. Wellington fell back, stopping to fight a delaying action at Busaco, but as Massena's men began their advance, thousands of Portuguese workers, organised by British officers, were busy frantically putting the finishing touches to a set of forts, redoubts and other obstacles. When linked together, these formed the remarkably successful Lines of Torres Vedras, three lines of fortifications which Wellington had ordered built as early as October 1809; almost a year to the day afterwards, they were occupied by the Allied army. Massena was stunned by their appearance and, after a brief flirtation with the Lines at Sobral, made no attempt to force them; his army simply sat down in front of them for the next four weeks until, after stripping the countryside bare, they withdrew to Santarem in need of food. By the following March the situation had not improved at all for Massena, and on 5 March he began to withdraw to the north, followed all the way by Wellington. On 3 April 1811, following their defeat at Sabugal, the French were thrown back into Spain. Never again would they invade Portugal.

The following month saw the Allies before the walls of Badajoz, the immensely strong fortress town which commanded the southern corridor between Portugal and Spain. This had to be taken from the French before any Allied advance into Spain could be contemplated. The first siege, in May 1811, was broken off when Marshal Soult marched from the south to relieve the town and on 16 May fought the Allies, under Beresford, at Albuera. The battle was one of the bloodiest of the war, and was decided by the outstanding courage of the British infantry, who refused to be driven from the field in spite of massive French attacks. Beresford resumed the siege of Badajoz in June, but was thwarted by a brave and tenacious French garrison, who saw off the British attacks,

BELOW **The camp at Villa Velha, after a painting by Thomas St Clair. A wonderful picture of army life in the Peninsula, painted by an eye-witness who saw action with the Portuguese army.**

ABOVE **The bridge over the Ebro at San Martin de Lines, crossed by Graham's troops on 14 June during the advance to Vittoria. This picture was taken from the southern bank of the Ebro.**

inflicting heavy casualties. Wellington had been involved in a similarly hard fight 13 days earlier at Fuentes de Onoro. Ostensibly it had been an attempt by Massena to relieve the garrison of Almeida, which was being blockaded by the Allies. The attempt failed, however, and Massena was recalled to Paris, never to return to Spain.

The year 1811 ended with a series of moves and counter-moves by both armies, until by December Wellington and his army were camped to the west of Ciudad Rodrigo, the fortress town which controlled the northern corridor between Spain and Portugal. It came as something of a surprise to the French governor, Barrie, when Wellington turned up on his doorstep on the bitterly cold morning of 8 January 1812. Eleven days later Barrie and those of his garrison who had not been killed during the siege or storming were prisoners-of-war, the town having fallen to Wellington's men on the night of 19 January.

Wellington's army slipped away to Badajoz soon afterwards, the commander-in-chief himself following on 5 March, and 11 days later the Allies began their investment of the town. The siege was to be a thoroughly miserable one for the Allies, with heavy rain making digging almost impossible, but eventually, on 6 April, the breaches were declared practicable and orders were issued for the assault. The storming of Badajoz is one of the bloodiest episodes in the long history of the British army. It is estimated that some 40 attacks were made against the breaches, all of which failed. Amazingly, the two diversionary attacks succeeded and the town was won, but at an enormous cost – nearly 4,000 British and Portuguese casualties.

With both Ciudad Rodrigo and Badajoz in Allied hands, Wellington could contemplate an advance into Spain. Before he could do so, however, Marmont, the new French commander in the Peninsula, moved against Ciudad Rodrigo, causing Wellington to return north. The

LEFT **The perpendicular rocks to the south-west of San Millan through which Maucune's 2nd Brigade emerged, bringing it into the rear of Vandeleur's brigade of the Light Division.**

BELOW **A view of the battlefield of San Millan, taken from the hills to the east of the village. The road on the right of this picture was the route taken by the Light Division. It came across Maucune's leading brigade resting in the fields by the trees on the right. Vandeleur's brigade chased the French through the village up onto the hill from where this picture was taken. Maucune's second brigade then emerged from the gap in the rocks on the left, taking the road that runs from it. It was then attacked itself by Kempt's brigade, forcing it to turn off the road and take to the fields on the left of this picture before being pursued with great loss over the hills behind out of picture to the left.**

threat was averted, and by June 1812 all was ready for an advance east. Wellington reached Salamanca on 17 June and on 22 July, after a couple of weeks of manoeuvring by both armies, he crushed Marmont at the battle of Salamanca. Never again would the French call him a defensive-minded and cautious commander. He had gained a reputation for being cautious as he was careful to preserve his army, which was the only one Britain could put into the field and his cautious tactics had been to prevent avoidable losses.

On 12 August Wellington entered Madrid amid much celebration. However, there was to be no swift end to the war: just three months later Wellington's army would be licking its wounds after the disastrous siege of Burgos in September and October and the subsequent retreat from there, which ended at Ciudad Rodrigo, the town from which Wellington had advanced with such high expectations that June. The winter of 1812/13 was spent recovering from the ordeal; those who had also been with Sir John Moore at Corunna were said to have had by far the worse of the two retreats. But by the spring of 1813 Wellington's men had regained their former strength, and with reinforcements that had been poured in from Britain hopes were high for a decisive campaign that year. They were not to be disappointed.

WELLINGTON BIDS FAREWELL TO PORTUGAL, MAY 1813

One of the most poignant moments of the war for Wellington came when his army set out from Portugal to begin its march north-east, a march that would culminate in the battle of Vittoria. After years of hard campaigning, during which he had thwarted three French invasions of Portugal and spent a great deal of time campaigning, he must have developed a great fondness for the country. Now, however, his army was fit and fully recovered from the trials and tribulations of the retreat from Burgos and he knew that the forthcoming campaign would decide the war in the Peninsula and that he would not be returning. Accompanied by some of his staff, Wellington turned in his saddle and, raising his cocked hat in the air, said, 'Farewell, Portugal, I shall never see you again'. He never did. (Bill Younghusband)

THE PENINSULAR WAR: CHRONOLOGY

1807

18 October	French troops cross the Spanish frontier.
30 November	Junot occupies Lisbon.

1808

23 March	The French occupy Madrid.
14 July	The French, under Bessières, defeat the Spaniards, under Cuesta and Blake, at Medina del Rio Seco.
22 July	The French surrender at Baylen.
1 August	A British force, under Sir Arthur Wellesley, lands at Mondego Bay, Portugal.
21 August	Wellesley defeats Junot at Vimeiro.
30 August	Convention of Cintra: Wellesley recalled to England.
30 October	The French evacuate Portugal.
8 November	Napoleon enters Spain with 200,000 men.
4 December	Napoleon occupies Madrid.
December	Moore advances from Salamanca.
21 December	British cavalry victory at Sahagun.

1809

16 January	Moore killed at Battle of Corunna.
22 April	Wellesley returns to Portugal.
12 May	Wellesley crosses the Douro and captures Oporto.
28-29 July	Wellesley defeats Joseph at Talavera.
4 September	Wellesley is created Viscount Wellington.

1810

10 July	Massena takes Ciudad Rodrigo.
24 July	Craufurd defeated by Ney on the Coa River.
27 September	Wellington victorious at Busaco.
10 October	Wellington enters the Lines of Torres Vedras.
14 October	Massena discovers Lines and halts.
17 November	Massena withdraws to Santarem.

1811

10 March	Soult takes Badajoz.
3-5 May	Wellington defeats Massena at Fuentes de Oñoro.
6 May	First British siege of Badajoz.
11 May	Brennier abandons Almeida to Wellington.
16 May	Beresford defeats Soult at Albuera.
19 May -17 June	Second British siege of Badajoz.

1812

8 January	Siege of Ciudad Rodrigo begins.
19 January	Wellington takes Ciudad Rodrigo by storm.
6-7 April	Wellington takes Badajoz by storm.
22 July	Wellington defeats Marmont at Salamanca.
12 August	Wellington enters Madrid.
19 September	Wellington begins siege of Burgos.
22 October	Wellington abandons siege of Burgos.
22 Oct.-19 Nov.	Allied retreat to Portugal.
19 November	Allied army arrives at Ciudad Rodrigo.

1813

3 June	Allied army crosses the Douro
13 June	French forces abandon Burgos
17 June	Wellington crosse the Ebro
18 June	Skirmish at San Millan
20 June	Allies halt and position themselves at Subjiana de Morillas
21 June	Wellington defeats Joseph at Vittoria, created Field Marshal.
25 July	Soult makes counterattack in the Pyrenees. Battles at Maya and Roncesvalles.
28-30 July	Wellington defeats Soult at Sorauren.
31 August	Graham takes San Sebastian by storm.
31 August	Soult repulsed at San Marcial.
7 October	Wellington crosses the Bidassoa into France.
25 October	Pamplona surrenders.
10 November	Wellington defeats Soult at the Battle of the Nivelle.
9-12 December	Wellington defeats Soult at the Battle of the Nive.
13 December	Soult repulsed by Hill at St Pierre.

1814

27 February	Wellington defeats Soult at Orthes.
6 April	Napoleon abdicates.
10 April	Wellington defeats Soult at Toulouse.
14 April	French sortie from Bayonne.
17 April	Soult surrenders.
27 April	Bayonne surrenders.
30 April	Treaty of Paris.
3 May	Wellington created Duke.

THE VITTORIA CAMPAIGN

The siege of Burgos had ended in an inglorious retreat to Portugal in November 1812 and it seemed the hard-won gains of that year had been in vain. Indeed, the opinion shared by more than a few of Wellington's officers was that Spain was lost for good, and that they might as well pack up and go home. It was not, however, a view shared by Wellington, and the Vittoria campaign of 1813 saw him bounce back with a vengeance.

Given the arduous nature of the retreat, Wellington's army recovered with remarkable speed and by the end of 1812 it was well on the way to regaining full strength. This was helped by the arrival of the first batch of reinforcements from England – a brigade of the Household Cavalry, numbering around 350 men, followed in February 1813 by a brigade of hussars from the 10th, 15th and 18th Hussars. Infantry reinforcements followed, and since the total number of recruits at home in 1812 exceeded the number of casualties in the Peninsula by 2,000, the army was not in short supply. In addition to the reinforcements sent out from England, Wellington fought and won his battle to retain his so-called 'provisional' battalions. These units were formed of the amalgamated skeleton battalions which had been reduced by either sickness or action. Rather than send home a weak battalion of, for example, 200 men, Wellington amalgamated it with a similar weak battalion to form a

BELOW **The battle of Vittoria. This French drawing shows Allied troops crossing what appear to be the bridges of Tres Puentes and, furthest away, Mendoza. This somewhat stylised picture is curiously accurate in one way in that it shows the ruined Roman temple which is situated on the knoll of Iruna above Tres Puentes.**

provisional battalion. He reasoned that experienced Peninsular troops were of greater value than 'green' troops from England, who were also prone to sickness – something which he could not afford with such an important campaign looming. The Duke of York, however, set himself against this practice and ordered that the weak battalions be brought home, mainly because it allowed the returning troops to recruit and bring the battalion back to full strength. There were never any provisional cavalry regiments, but in view of the large number of cavalry reinforcements being sent out to Spain, the Duke of York also gave orders that two under-strength cavalry regiments be brought home, after giving their horses to other regiments remaining in the Peninsula. It was a tough battle for Wellington, but he eventually won, although he did allow one provisional battalion and four cavalry regiments to return home.

The various army departments, particularly the Quartermaster General's and the Commissariat, underwent review and reorganisation of sorts and were in a much more effective condition for the coming campaign, while Wellington's senior officers were put under the spotlight as he set about ridding himself of several of the more troublesome and inefficient. Indeed, by the end of December the Peninsular army had seen the recall of Long, Erskine and Slade – three of its greatest characters – with Victor Alten, Low, Chowne and Bernewitz following a few weeks later. Erskine, in fact, committed suicide before he returned to England, while Long and Victor Alten, although taking part in the Vittoria campaign, left the Peninsula afterwards. The recall of such unwanted officers was, however, tempered by the appointment of some of their replacements, notably Fane and Rebow, who commanded the two new cavalry brigades.

The most important change of personnel was the replacing of the quartermaster general, Willoughby Gordon, with George Murray. Much of the blame for the 1812 retreat from Burgos lay at the feet of Gordon, and Wellington was keen to be rid of him. However, he was a great favourite at Horse Guards, and it would take some doing. The problem was solved when Gordon returned home sick at the end of 1812 and was diagnosed as needing an operation to cure him. This would prevent him from returning to the Peninsula for many months. The way was now open for the return of George Murray, a vastly underrated officer whose talents had a great influence on the course and conduct of the war. Indeed, it is no exaggeration to state that Murray was the key figure in Wellington's army after the commander-in-chief himself, and Wellington considered Murray his right-hand man.

Among the senior infantry officers, no fewer than eight of Wellington's tried and trusted generals were still in England at the end of 1812, most on sick leave. They included Graham, Picton, Pack, Brisbane, Byng, Leith, Cotton and Houston. Happily, all but the last three named officers returned to take part in the Vittoria campaign, with both Picton and Graham playing a major role in the battle. Wellington could, therefore, be fairly satisfied with his Allied army on the eve of the campaign. As to his own situation, he was appointed commander-in-chief of the Spanish army by the Spanish Cortes on 18 November 1812. It is not my intention to discuss the long, drawn-out saga accompanying the appointment, other than to say that it caused Wellington much grief, despite its undoubted advantages.

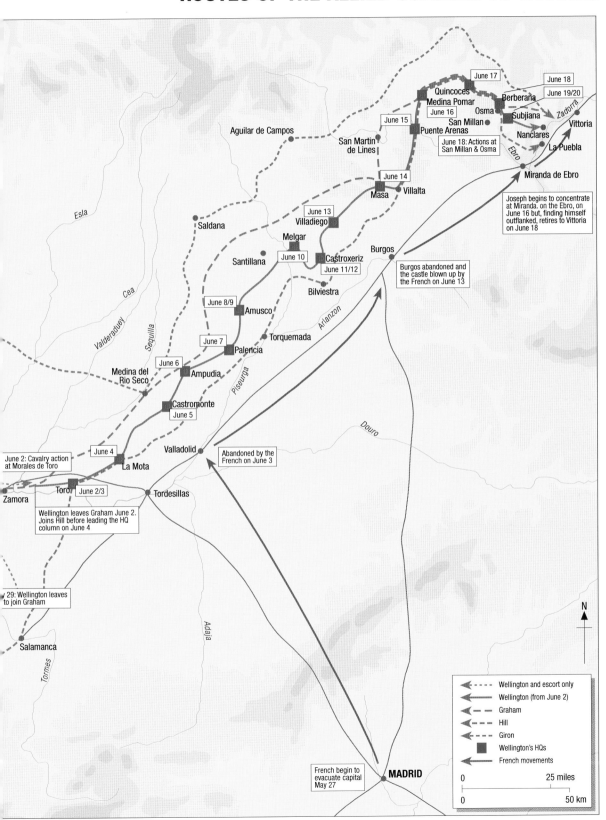

June 17

June 18

June 19/20

Quincoces

Medina Pomar

Berberaña

June 16

Osma

San Millan

Subjiana

Zadorra

Aguilar de Campos

June 15

San Martin
de Lines

Puente Arenas

Vittoria

Nanclares

La Puebla

June 18: Actions at
San Millan & Osma

June 14

Miranda de Ebro

Masa

Villalta

Esla

Joseph begins to concentrate
at Miranda. on the Ebro, on
June 16 but, finding himself
outflanked, retires to Vittoria
on June 18

Saldana

June 13

Villadiego

Melgar

June 10

Burgos

Santillana

Castroxeriz

June 11/12

Burgos abandoned and
the castle blown up by
the French on June 13

Cea

Bilviestra

June 8/9

Amusco

Arlanzon

Torquemada

June 7

Palencia

Piseurga

June 6

Medina del
Rio Seco

Ampudia

Castromonte

June 5

Douro

Valderaduey

Sequilla

Valladolid

Abandoned by the
French on June 3

June 4

June 2: Cavalry action
at Morales de Toro

La Mota

Toro

June 2/3

Tordesillas

Zamora

Wellington leaves Graham June 2.
Joins Hill before leading the HQ
column on June 4

Adaja

29: Wellington leaves
to join Graham

N

Salamanca

Tormes

	Wellington and escort only
	Wellington (from June 2)
	Graham
	Hill
	Giron
■	Wellington's HQs
	French movements

French begin to
evacuate capital
May 27

MADRID

0   25 miles

0   50 km

By early May 1813 Wellington's army had fully recovered from the trials and traumas of the previous campaign and was in great strength, morally and physically. The same could not be said of the French, however, for Napoleon had begun to recall French troops for the coming campaign in Germany. Some 15,000 troops had been withdrawn from Spain by February 1813. Coupled with increased threats from Spanish guerrillas, which, crucially, diverted the attentions of thousands of other French troops, this seriously weakened the French armies facing Wellington when he began the Vittoria campaign. Coupled with this was the recall to Paris of senior French commanders including Soult and Caffarelli, commander of the Army of the North. One other reason which undoubtedly hampered the French was the interference from Paris by Napoleon himself, whose grasp of the real situation in the Peninsula left much to be desired and seriously hampered his brother's attempts to retain some degree of control over his own situation. Indeed, Napoleon appears to have been way out of touch with the state of affairs in Spain, his intelligence both from the Peninsula and from his spies in England – not to mention the English press – led him to seriously underrate the strength of Wellington's army, both in numbers and in morale, so much so that he was convinced that Wellington would not be able to put into the field more than 50,000 British and Portuguese troops during the coming campaign.

Against them were just under 70,000 French troops from the Armies of the South, Centre and Portugal, whose positions in March 1813 were thus: the Army of the South (just under 35,000 men) was placed between Madrid and the Douro, with Joseph having abandoned the capital in favour of Valladolid; the Army of the Centre (17,000 troops) occupied the province of Segovia; and the Army of Portugal (also around 17,000) was sent north to deal with the Spanish insurrection in the Basque country. Indeed, the trouble in the north would have grave consequences for the French during the Vittoria campaign. This is best illustrated by the fact that the redoubtable General Foy and his division, instead of marching to Joseph's aid, found themselves engaged against Spanish guerrillas; they were to be sorely missed. Furthermore – and more crucially – was the absence on 21 June 1813 of Clausel and the Army of the North, whose 20,000 men would have been mightily useful to Joseph at Vittoria had they not been busy around Pamplona, again chasing Spanish brigands and bandits.

Wellington himself had thought long and hard about his plan of campaign and by the end of March 1813 he was in a position to set a start date of 1 May. The plan was an ambitious one which, if successful, would drive the French all the way to the Pyrenees. Wellington's optimism increased as he received reports that pointed to a steady weakening of his enemies, as drafts and generals were sent to Germany. All factors indicated to him that he would never be in a better position to bring the war to a decisive and satisfactory conclusion.

Wellington's plan involved an advance by his army in two wings, the left under Sir Thomas Graham with six divisions, and the right under Hill with three divisions. Graham was to cross the Douro well inside Portugal at Braganza and Miranda, the move being set for 21-24 May. Hill, meanwhile, was to move north from his headquarters at Coria and advance on Salamanca. Upon arrival he was to march to his left and head

ABOVE **Today, the river Esla at Almendra is a far cry from the state it was in back in 1813 owing to a dam which has been built to the south. The river was once 'as wide as the Thames at Windsor' and when Graham's column crossed it on 31 May it was in full flood, many British infantrymen being drowned while crossing it despite the efforts of the cavalry who brought many of them across, the infantry holding on to their stirrups as they went. Large amounts of equipment were lost also. The ford from the village can easily be seen leading down to the river but the width and depth of the water have changed dramatically.**

for the Douro at Toro. There he would join with Graham, who by then should have crossed the Esla north of Zamora and in so doing would complete the concentration of Wellington's army. More important, however, was the fact that once the two wings had established themselves on the north bank of the Douro, they would have turned the right wing of the French position on the Douro without having had to engage in a single serious action. The advance would either bring on a general engagement in front of Joseph's capital, Valladolid, or force Joseph to retire upon Burgos. The sweep north of the great road to France would also allow Wellington to move his supply line from Lisbon to northern Spain, a feat which the French thought highly improbable.

First of all, Hill had to gather together his own wing of the army which was spread over a wide area, ranging from as far south as the Tagus, south of which were Morillo's Spaniards, to the old ground on the Coa and Agueda rivers, where the Light Division had spent yet another winter. There were also the cavalry brigades of Victor Alten, Fane and Robert Hill, the latter being the newly arrived Household Brigade. These three had to march from Lisbon to join Hill around Ciudad Rodrigo. On 22 May Wellington left his old headquarters at Freneida for the last time and rode to join Hill at Ciudad Rodrigo. Two days later the southern wing of the army had concentrated, and a further two days saw the Allies closing in on Salamanca, which was being tardily evacuated by Villatte. So slow was he in leaving the town, that he was caught by British cavalry

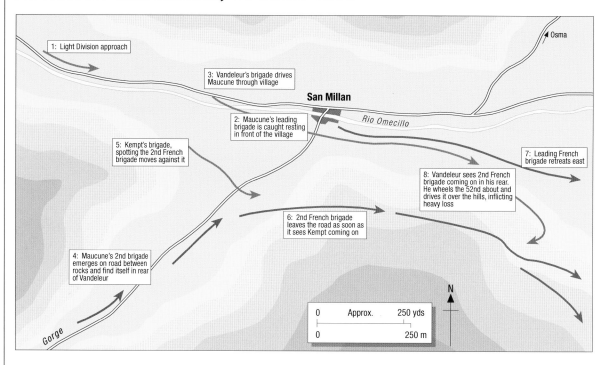

which, although unable to break into the French rearguard, managed to round up over 200 prisoners. Salamanca was, therefore, back in Allied hands. Wellington's presence at Salamanca went a long way to convincing the French that the main body of the Allied army was there with him, just as Wellington had hoped, yet in fact only one third of his army was with him. From here onwards, the French were chasing shadows, unaware of the great strength of Graham's wing of the army and convinced that the main threat to them would come along the great road through Tordesillas, Valladolid and Burgos.

No sooner had Wellington secured Salamanca than he left Hill's wing of the army and made a swift ride north across rough tracks to join Graham, who was preparing to cross the Esla with the main body of the Allied army. Hill, meanwhile, was to push on to the Douro at Toro. Wellington left Salamanca on 29 May and the following day arrived at Graham's headquarters at Carvajales, to find the army faced with the problem of crossing the river. The Esla was in full flood when the troops crossed opposite Almendra on 31 May, and many men were drowned. Indeed, it was only by hanging on to the stirrups of the cavalry that many of them reached the other side. So much equipment was lost during the crossing that it is said that for weeks afterwards, whenever there was an inspection, men who had sold equipment to the locals for drinking money simply said they had lost it in the Esla! The French were certainly tardy in watching the river, and Graham's wing crossed without any interference.

The appearance of Graham's wing on the right bank of the Esla was received with great shock by Joseph and Jourdan, the king's chief-of-staff, who quickly pulled back from the Douro without putting up any resistance. Hence the great barrier of the Douro – the main French defensive line – had been passed as if it were a village stream. As Graham's force marched east, his cavalry began to encounter enemy units, and on 2 June they achieved a notable success at Morales de Toro, when the 10th, 15th and 18th Hussars charged and drove off an enemy force of the 16th Dragoons. The victory was one of a series of well managed actions by British cavalry in the Peninsula – Benavente, Sahagun, Villagarcia, Los Santos, Usagre included, not to mention success during major battles such as Salamanca.

By 3 June Wellington's entire army was secure on the northern bank of the Douro, forcing the French to retreat north to Valladolid. However, if Joseph and Jourdan entertained ideas of holding the Allies there, they were to be sadly disappointed, as Wellington kept his line of march to the north of the great road, thus outflanking the French once again. The French retired yet again, this time to Burgos, the scene of Wellington's one and only great failure in the Peninsula. It had eluded his grasp in September and October of 1812, and his failure to take it had led to the great retreat of October and November, which ended with the Allies back on the Portuguese border. This time there was to be no retreat, for on 13 June the French garrison abandoned the castle and simply blew it up.

Wellington now faced the most difficult terrain of the whole advance, the country being mountainous and criss-crossed by gorges and good defensive positions. Indeed, the area to the north of Burgos is unlike any other part of Spain, with wooded plateaux fringed with sheer drops and ravines; it is a most spectacular part of the country. It was also terrain through which the French thought it impossible to bring guns and wagons. However, Wellington, very daringly, chose to attempt it, and before long the three great Allied columns were snaking their way through the mountain roads and paths, Hill just to the north of the great road, Graham and Wellington on his left, deep within the mountains, and Giron's Spaniards

ABOVE **Subjiana de Morillos, Wellington's headquarters on the eve of the battle of Vittoria. The river is the Bayas.**

further to the west. The advance gave Wellington three great advantages.

First, by maintaining a good pace and keeping to the mountains, Wellington avoided following directly in the footsteps of the retreating French. This latter course would have slowed him down owing to the number of good defensive positions, such as Pancorbo, along the way. Any delay would inevitably have allowed Clausel and the Army of the North, marching to Joseph's aid, to join the French and give them a great numerical superiority.

Secondly, once he had crossed the Ebro, Wellington could shift his communications to the ports of northern Spain and thus avoid being overstretched. Some supplies had already been landed at Corunna but as the army moved north-east, Wellington was able to use Santander and thus end his reliance upon Lisbon. The French thought it highly unlikely that Wellington would be able to do this, indeed, Jourdan had even advocated a plan of action which involved a strike against Wellington's lines of communications – to Lisbon! This clearly demonstrates just how much they underestimated Wellington and how little they knew of his real movements.

Thirdly, Wellington's march through the mountains continued his policy of outflanking the French positions. Indeed, when, on the evening of 17 June, Allied cavalry clashed with the enemy – their first contact for four days – the French realised that Wellington had got round the right flank of their supposedly strong position on the Ebro. The lack of good intelligence on the French side was a great factor in their downfall, and it is remarkable that for four days they had no idea of Wellington's whereabouts. Cavalry patrols were sent out but, fortunately for Wellington, they appear to have halted a village too soon on each occasion and to have reported back that the Allies were nowhere to be found. It seems almost certain that Joseph and his subordinates placed far too much faith in the impossibility of passing through the mountainous region to the north of the great road. The line of the Ebro, for example, was turned before the French realised it, Graham's troops pouring over the Ebro at San Martin de Lines and Hill's at the Puente Arenas.

Contact was, however, inevitable and on 18 June there was a sharp fight at the small village of San Millan, when the Light Division came across one of General Maucune's brigades resting in front of the village. While Vandeleur's brigade was driving it beyond the village, a second French brigade appeared from a rocky track behind them. This was charged by Kempt's brigade of the Light Division, thus creating the strange spectacle of one French brigade being pursued by a British brigade which was in turn being pursued by a French brigade being pursued by another British brigade! As soon as the leading British unit, the 52nd, saw what was happening behind it, the men wheeled round, apparently at running pace, and opened fire on the second French brigade, driving it over the hills and inflicting some 400 casualties. So furious was Joseph at Maucune's conduct in allowing himself to be badly mauled, that he ordered Maucune's division back to France in charge of part of the great convoy that had gathered at Vittoria. Thus these troops were wasted, and they were to be missed on 21 June. The French tried to make a stand at Osma the same day, but this was effortlessly beaten back and with it went Joseph's last chance of protecting his right flank. His position on the Ebro was given up, and he continued east along the great road to Vittoria.

Such was the chaos within the French army that the prisoners taken by Wellington at San Millan had no idea of the whereabouts of Clausel; neither did Joseph or Jourdan, who had sent out scouts in every direction in a desperate attempt to find him. Wellington, on the other hand, knew exactly where Clausel was, owing to the wonderful network of 'correspondents' which he had painstakingly set up over the long years of the war. From intelligence received from his spies, Wellington knew that Clausel was still at Pamplona on 16 June, and given that it would take at least six days for them to reach Vittoria, Wellington realised that he had to fight the French before 22 June. Furthermore, Wellington's correspondents had informed him that such was the size of the convoy which had collected in Vittoria that it would take days to get it clear. General Rey had left Vittoria for San Sebastian with part of the great convoy, but the greater part of it remained behind. As we shall see, its presence was to have an important bearing on the outcome of the battle. On 20 June Wellington halted at Subjiana de Morillas, on the river Bayas, to concentrate his forces and make his final plans for the attack on Joseph at Vittoria.

ABOVE **One of Cruikshank's comments on Wellington's victory. Wellington is presented with Jourdan's 'rolling pin', his marshal's baton. Wellington sent it to the Prince Regent who promptly created him a Field Marshal. No French eagles were captured at Vittoria despite Cruikshank's depiction of such in this cartoon.**

WELLINGTON

The key personality at the battle of Vittoria was Arthur Wellesley (1769-1852), later to become 1st Duke of Wellington. He had been raised to the peerage in September 1809 following his victory at Talavera on 27/28 July. Created Viscount Wellington of Talavera, this was followed in February 1812 by an earldom. He was also created a Grandee of Spain, with the title of Duque de Ciudad Rodrigo. In March 1813 he was made Knight of the Garter, and following the battle of Vittoria he had other honours conferred upon him.

Wellington had come out to the Peninsula in late July 1808 and by the end of the following month had twice beaten the French – at Rolica and Vimeiro – and had seen his enemies thrown out of Portugal following the Convention of Cintra. However, the convention had not been favoured by the British public, and he had been recalled to face a court of enquiry along with Sir Hew Dalrymple and Sir Harry Burrard, both of whom had superseded him following the battle of Vimeiro. Acquitted of all charges, Wellington – although he had yet to win the title – returned to Portugal and did not leave until the French were finally defeated in the Peninsula in 1814. During that time he forged one of the finest armies Britain has ever possessed, one with which Wellington later said he could 'go

LEFT **Arthur Wellesley, 1st Duke of Wellington (1769-1852). The key figure in the Peninsular War, Wellesley was created Viscount Wellington of Talavera following his victory there in July 1809. Apart from one short interval when he returned home to England to face the Court of Inquiry following the Convention of Cintra in 1808, Wellington commanded the Anglo-Portuguese army in the Peninsula throughout the war without a single day's leave, until he returned to England in 1814. He was created a Duke in May 1814 and fought his last campaign the following year, when, with the aid of his Prussian allies, he defeated Napoleon at Waterloo.**

LEFT **General Miguel Alava (1771-1843). Alava was a native of Vittoria and his local knowledge was of great use to Wellington during the campaign. Alava was not only Wellington's Spanish liaison officer but was one of the most trusted of his subordinates. He had served with the Spaniards at Trafalgar and later fought alongside Wellington at Waterloo.**

anywhere and do anything'. In addition to the three victories already won in 1808 and 1809, Wellington defeated the French at Oporto, Busaco, Fuentes de Onoro, Salamanca, the Pyrenees, the Nivelle, Nive, Orthes and – somewhat controversially – at Toulouse. He also gained the fortresses of Ciudad Rodrigo and Badajoz, and won a series of smaller actions during the defeat of Massena's third invasion of Portugal in 1811. The battle of Vittoria was probably the most crushing victory, and was the one which effectively brought an end to French aspirations in the Peninsula. Of course Wellington also commanded the Anglo-Dutch army which defeated Napoleon at Waterloo on 18 June 1815.

Wellington was blessed with having a more than able army commanded by very skilful lieutenants. Of these, none was more adept at independent command than Sir Rowland Hill (1772-1842). He was affectionately known as 'Daddy' Hill by his men, mostly those of the 2nd Division, which he commanded

LEFT **Sir Thomas Picton (1758-1815). Picton commanded the 'Fighting' 3rd Division at Vittoria and it was his attack on the bridge of Mendoza which pierced the centre of the French line. One of the great characters in Wellington's army, he was to die leading his men at Waterloo in 1815.**

for a great part of the war. Hill won two notable victories over the French: at Arroyomolinos in October 1811, and at Almaraz in May 1812. He commanded the right wing of Wellington's army during the battle of the Nive and achieved a notable success at St Pierre on 13 December 1813. Hill became commander-in-chief of the army in 1825. At Vittoria, he commanded the right wing of Wellington's army.

Lieutenant General Sir George Ramsay, Earl Dalhousie (1770-1838), commanded the 7th Division at Vittoria. This division had only been created in 1811, while Dalhousie himself had not gone out to the Peninsula until 1812. He never really displayed any great brilliance in the field and proved a fairly ordinary divisional commander. The timing of his arrival at Vittoria had a significant effect on the course of the battle, as we shall see. Wellington gave Dalhousie command of one of the central columns of the army at Vittoria over the head of Sir Thomas Picton (1758-1815), which perhaps shows that Wellington considered him reliable enough for the task.

Picton himself was one of the great firebrands in Wellington's army. He was as brave as a lion and had served in the Peninsula since 1810. He commanded the 'fighting' 3rd Division, and was wounded while leading it against the formidable walls of the castle of Badajoz in April 1812. Picton was criticised by Wellington for his behaviour following the battle of Roncesvalles in July 1813, when, like Sir Lowry Cole, his nerve appeared to have deserted him, prompting Wellington to write that although his commanders were like heroes when he himself was present, when he was absent they were prone to 'behave like children'. Picton died at the head of his men at Waterloo in 1815, a fitting end for such a gallant fighter.

The left wing of the Allied army at Vittoria was commanded by Sir Thomas Graham, one of the great characters of the Peninsular War. Graham (1748-1843) did not join the British army until he was 46 years old. His wife had died while they were in France, and when French revolutionary guards forced him to open his wife's coffin – apparently looking for illegal arms –

LEFT **Sir Thomas Graham (1748-1843). Graham commanded the left wing of Wellington's army during the advance to Vittoria. Never really convincing during the battle itself, he has often been criticised for not pushing harder against the French right flank. He was an experienced fighter and had won the battle of Barrosa in 1811. He was plagued by eye trouble, however, which finally compelled him to leave the Peninsula in 1813. He later became Lord Lynedoch.**

LEFT **General Francisco Longa (1770-1831). Longa's Spanish division attacked the village of Durana during the battle and achieved the cutting of the great road to France, one of the main Allied objectives during the battle.**

BELOW **General Pablo Morillo. One of the heroes of the battle of Vittoria, Morillo was badly wounded whilst leading his Spanish division against the French defenders on the heights of Puebla.**

Graham vowed to raise his own regiment to fight the French. He did so in the Peninsula with great success, and was the victor of the battle of Barrosa in March 1811. He served with Sir John Moore during the Corunna campaign of 1808/9 and commanded the Allied force which stormed San Sebastian in August 1813. He later became Lord Lynedoch.

Serving alongside Graham at Vittoria was General Francisco Longa (1770-1831), one of the former guerrilla leaders who acted virtually as an auxiliary for a great part of the war. Indeed, Longa later commanded a division in the Spanish army. Another Spanish commander to serve with distinction at Vittoria was General Pablo Morillo, who fought alongside Rowland Hill with the right wing of Wellington's army on the Puebla heights. Morillo later served with distinction in South America during the wars of independence there following the close of the Peninsular War.

THE FRENCH

BELOW **Marshal Jean Baptiste, Count Jourdan (1762-1833). Jourdan was chief of staff to King Joseph and must take a large slice of the blame for the French defeat at Vittoria. Indeed, he was sacked soon afterwards.**

The French army at Vittoria was nominally under the command of Napoleon's brother, Joseph (1768-1844). Joseph, or 'Tio Pepe' as the Spaniards called him, had been installed as King of Spain in 1808 and had ruled fairly ever since. He was no great commander of armies, however, and following his defeat at Vittoria, he returned to France. Despite the presence of Joseph Bonaparte, the French army at Vittoria was, in reality, directed by Joseph's chief of staff, Marshal Jean-Baptiste Jourdan (1762-1833), was an experienced soldier who had seen action in the American War of Independence. Created a marshal in 1804, he had served as chief of staff to Joseph in 1808 and from 1812 to 1813, and it was he, rather than Joseph, whom Napoleon later blamed for the defeat at Vittoria.

One of the main culprits for the disaster in Vittoria, however, was General Honore Theodore Maxime Gazan (1765-1845). Gazan had seen widespread service in the Peninsula from 1808 and had led both the Army of Andalucia – which he commanded at Vittoria – and the Army of the Centre. He was later to serve as chief of staff to the Army of the Pyrenees. Gazan's role on the battlefield of Vittoria had a crucial effect on the outcome of the battle.

General Honore Charles Michale Joseph, Comte de Reille (1775-1860), was another very experienced French soldier who had seen great service in the Peninsula. At Vittoria he commanded the Army of Portugal, and he emerged from the battle with his reputation relatively unscathed. He later fought at Waterloo, was made a Marshal of France in 1847, and outlived most of his contemporaries.

Command of the Army of the Centre at Vittoria lay with General Jean-Baptiste, Count D'Erlon (1765-1844). Another Peninsular veteran, D'Erlon had served in Spain since 1810 and had, at various stages, commanded both the Army of Portugal and the Army of the Centre; the latter he commanded at Vittoria. D'Erlon was later to command a corps at Waterloo, and was made a Marshal of France in 1843.

These were the main figures at Vittoria, but there were many other brigade and battalion commanders on both sides who were to fight – and die – bravely on 21 June 1813.

RIGHT **General Jean Baptiste, Count D'Erlon (1765-1844), commander of the Army of the Centre at Vittoria. D'Erlon was one of Napoleon's most durable generals in the Peninsula and was a corps commander at Waterloo in 1815.**

ORDER OF BATTLE

ALLIED FORCES

BRITISH TROOPS

CAVALRY

	Officers	Men	Total
R Hill's Brigade: 1st and 2nd Life Guards, Horse Guards	42	828	870
Ponsonby's Brigade: 5th Dragoon Guards, 3rd and 4th Dragoons	61	1,177	1,238
G. Anson's Brigade: 12th and 16th Light Dragoons	39	780	819
Long's Brigade: 13th Light Dragoons	20	374	394
V. Alten's Brigade: 14th Light Dragoons, 1st Hussars KGL	49	956	1,005
Bock's Brigade: 1st and 2nd Dragoons, KGL	38	594	632
Fane's Brigade: 3rd Dragoon Guards, 1st Dragoons	42	800	842
Grant's Brigade: 10th, 15th, 18th Hussars	63	1,561	1,624
D'Urban's Portuguese Brigade: 1st, 11th, 12th Cavalry	–	685	685
6th Portuguese Cavalry	–	208	208
TOTAL	**354**	**7,963**	**8,317**

INFANTRY

1ST DIVISION, HOWARD

	Officers	Men	Total
Stopford Brigade: 1/Coldstream, 1/3rd Guards, 1 Coy 5/60th	56	1,672	1,728
Halkett's Brigade: 1st, 2nd, 5th Line KGL, 1st and 2nd Light KGL	133	2,993	3,126
TOTAL	**189**	**4,665**	**4,854**

2ND DIVISION, HILL

	Officers	Men	Total
Cadogan's Brigade: 1/50th, 1/71st, 1/92nd, 1 Coy 5/60th	120	2,657	2,777
Byng's Brigade: 1/3rd, 1/57th, 1st Prov. Batt. 1 Coy 5/60th	131	2,334	2,465
O'Callaghan's Brigade: 1/28th, 2/34th, 1/39th, 1 Coy 5/60th	122	2,408	2,530
TOTAL	**373**	**7,399**	**7,772**

3RD DIVISION, PICTON

	Officers	Men	Total
Brisbane's Brigade: 1/45th, 74th, 1/88th, 3 Coys 5/60th	125	2,598	2,723
Colville's Brigade: 1/5th, 2/83rd, 2/87th, 94th	120	2,156	2,276
Power's Portuguese Brigade: 9th and 21st Line, 11th Cacadores	–	2,460	2,460
TOTAL	**245**	**7,214**	**7,459**

4TH DIVISION, COLE

	Officers	Men	Total
W. Anson's Brigade: 3/27th, 1/40th, 1/48th, 2nd Prov. Batt. 1 Coy 5/60th	139	2,796	2,935
Skerrett's Brigade: 1/7th, 20th, 1/23rd, 1 Coy Brunswickers	123	1,926	2,045
Stubb's Portuguese Brigade: 11th and 23rd Line, 7th Cacadores	–	2,842	2,842
TOTAL	**262**	**7,564**	**7,826**

5TH DIVISION, OSWALD

	Officers	Men	Total
Hay's Brigade: 3/1st, 1/9th, 1/38th, 1 Coy Brunswickers	109	2,183	2,292
Robinson's Brigade: 1/4th, 2/47th, 2/59th, 1 Coy Brunswickers	100	1,961	2,061
Spry's Portuguese Brigade: 3rd and 15th Line, 8th Cacadores	–	2,372	2,372
TOTAL	**209**	**6,519**	**6,725**

6TH DIVISION, PAKENHAM

	Officers	Men	Total
Stirling's Brigade: 1/42nd, 1/79th, 1/91st, 1 Coy 5/60th	127	2,327	2,454
Hinde's Brigade: 1/11th, 1/32nd, 1/36th, 1/61st	130	2,288	2,418
Madden's Portuguese Brigade: 8th and 12th Line, 9th Cacadores	–	2,475	2,475
TOTAL	**257**	**7,090**	**7,347**

7TH DIVISION, DALHOUSIE

	Officers	Men	Total
Barnes's Brigade: 1/6th, 3rd Prov. Batt. 9 coys Brunswick Oels	116	2,206	2,322
Grant's Brigade: 51st, 68th, 1/82nd, Chasseurs Britanniques	141	2,397	2,538
Lecor's Portuguese Brigade: 7th and 19th Line, 2nd Cacadores	–	2,437	2,437
TOTAL	**287**	**7,040**	**7,297**

LIGHT DIVISION CHARLES ALTEN

	Officers	Men	Total
Kempt's Brigade: 1/43rd, 1/95th, 3/95th	98	1,979	2,077
Vandeleur's Brigade: 1/52nd, 2/95th	63	1,399	1,462
Portuguese 17th Line, 1st and 3rd Cacadores	–	1,945	1,945
TOTAL	**161**	**5,323**	**5,484**

PORTUGUESE DIVISION SILVEIRA'S

	Officers	Men	Total
Da Costa's Brigade: 2nd and 14th Line	–	2,492	2,492
A. Campbell's Brigade: 4th and 10th Line, 10th Cacadores	–	2,795	2,795
Pack's Portuguese Brigade: 1st and 16th Line, 4th Cacadores	–	2,297	2,297
Bradford's Portuguese Brigade: 13th and 24th Line, 5th Cacadores	–	2,392	2,392
TOTAL	**–**	**9,976**	**9,976**
RHA and Drivers	23	780	803
Field Artillery, Train, Ammunition Column etc.	100	2,722	2,822
KGL Artillery	17	335	352
Portuguese Artillery	–	330	330
Engineers and Sappers	41	302	343
Staff Corps	21	126	147
Wagon Train	37	165	202
TOTAL	**239**	**4,760**	**4,999**
TOTAL NUMBER OF BRITISH TROOPS	**2,576**	**76,276**	**78,852**

SPANISH TROOPS

MORILLO'S DIVISION

Officers	Men	Total
172	4,379	4,551

LOSADA'S GALICIAN DIVISION

	Officers	Men	Total
(6 Batts)	295	5,560	5,855

P. BARCENA'S GALICIAN DIVISION

	Officers	Men	Total
(7 Batts)	235	4,908	5,143

PORLIER'S ASTURIAN DIVISION

	Officers	Men	Total
(3 Batts)	124	2,284	2,408

LONGA'S DIVISION

	Officers	Men	Total
(5 Batts)	130	3,000	3,130

PENNE VILLEMUR'S CAVALRY

	Officers	Men	Total
(7 Regts)	194	2,434	2,628

JULIAN SANCHEZ'S CAVALRY

	Officers	Men	Total
(2 Regts)	90	1,200	1,290

ARTILLERY

Officers	Men	Total
20	400	240

	Officers	Men	Total
TOTAL NUMBER OF SPANISH TROOPS	**1,263**	**24,165**	**25,428**
TOTAL NUMBER OF ALLIED TROOPS	**3,839**	**100,441**	**104,280**

FRENCH FORCES

ARMY OF THE SOUTH

1ST DIVISION, LEVAL

	Officers	Men	Total
Mocquery's Brigade: 9th Leger, 24th Line	63	2,516	2,579
Morgan's Brigade: 88th Line, 96th Line	43	2,056	2,099
Divisional Battery and Train	3	163	166
Divisional Total	109	4,735	4,844

2ND DIVISION

Cassagne (lent to Army of the Centre)

3RD DIVISION, VILLATTE

	Officers	Men	Total
Rignoux's Brigade: 27th Leger, 63rd Line	39	2,539	2,578
Lefol's Brigade: 94th Line, 95th Line	50	3,063	3,113
Divisional Battery and Train	4	179	183
Divisional Total	93	5,781	5,874

4TH DIVISION, CONROUX

	Officers	Men	Total
Rey's Brigade: 32nd Line, 43rd Line	78	3,591	3,669
Schwitter's Brigade: 55th Line, 58th Line	47	2,670	2,717
Divisional Battery and Train	4	189	193
Divisional Total	129	6,460	6,589

5TH DIVISION, MARANSIN'S BRIGADE ONLY

	Officers	Men	Total
12th Leger, 45th Line	58	2,869	2,927

6TH DIVISION, DARICAU

	Officers	Men	Total
St Pol's Brigade: 21st Leger, 100th Line	53	2,658	2,711
Remond's Brigade: 28th Leger, 103rd Line	45	2,939	2,984
Divisional Battery and Train	3	237	240
Divisional Total	101	5,834	5,935
Total 4.5 Infantry Divisions	490	25,679	26,169

CAVALRY

PIERRE SOULT'S DIVISION

	Officers	Men	Total
2nd Hussars, 5th, 10th, 21st Chasseurs	74	1,428	1,502
1 Battery HA and Train	4	165	169

TILLY'S DIVISION

	Officers	Men	Total
2nd, 4th, 14th, 17th, 26th, 27th Dragoons	88	1,841	1,929

DIGEON'S DIVISION

	Officers	Men	Total
5th, 12th, 16th, 21st Dragoons	80	1,612	1,692
1 Battery HA and Train	3	174	177
Total Cavalry	249	6,220	6,469

AUXILIARY TROOPS

	Officers	Men	Total
Artillery Reserve: 2 Batteries, Train	5	365	370
Artillery Park: 2 Coys Field Artillery, 1 Coy Pontiniers, Artificers, Train	17	696	713
Engineers: 2 Coys Sappers, 2 Miners, Train	11	619	630
Gendarmerie	4	101	105
Wagon Train	2	63	65
Total Auxiliary Troops	39	1,844	1,883
Etat-Major of the Army and the Divisions	115	–	115
TOTAL OF THE ARMY OF THE SOUTH	893	33,743	34,636

ARMY OF THE CENTRE

1ST DIVISION, DARMAGNAC

	Officers	Men	Total
Chasse's Brigade: 28th Line, 75th Line	35	1,759	1,794
Nueunstein's Brigade: 2nd Nassau, 4th Baden, Franfort	101	2,577	2,678
Divisional Total	136	4,336	4,472

2ND DIVISION, CASSAGNE

	Officers	Men	Total
Braun's Brigade: 16th Leger 8th Line			
Blondeau's Brigade: 51st Line, 54th Line	95	5,114	5,209
Total Infantry	231	9,450	9,681

CAVALRY

TREILLARD'S DIVISION

	Officers	Men	Total
13th, 18th, 19th, 22nd Dragoons	44	994	1,038
Avy's Light Cavalry: 27th Chasseurs, Nassau Chasseurs	22	452	474
Total Cavalry	66	1,446	1,512

AUXILIARY TROOPS	Officers	Men	Total
Artillery: 3 Batteries, Train	13	488	501
Engineers: 1 Coy Sappers	2	129	131
Wagon Train etc.	3	195	198
Total Auxiliary Arms	28	812	830

THE KING'S SPANISH ARMY	Officers	Men	Total
Royal Guards, General Guy			
Grenadiers, Tirailleurs, Voltigeurs of the Guard	80	2,300	2,380
Hussars and Lancers of the Guard	25	400	425
Line: Regiments of Castile, Toledo, Royal Etranger	70	2,000	2,070
Cavalry: 1st and 2nd Chasseurs, Hussars of Guadalajara	70	600	670
Artillery: 1 Battery	3	90	93
Total King's Army	248	5,390	5,633
TOTAL ARMY OF THE CENTRE	603	17,098	17,691

ARMY OF PORTUGAL

4TH DIVISION, SARRUT

	Officers	Men	Total
Fririon's Brigade: 2nd Leger, 36th Line			
Menne's Brigade: 4th Leger, 65th Line			
Divisional Field Battery and Train	146	4,656	4,802

6TH DIVISION, LAMARTINIERE

	Officers	Men	Total
Gauthier's Brigade: 118th Line, 119th Line	71	2,496	2,567
Menne's Brigade: 120th Line, 122nd Line	102	3,866	3,968
Divisional Field Battery and Trail:	3	173	176
Total Infantry Divisions	322	11,191	11,513

CAVALRY

MERMET'S DIVISION

	Officers	Men	Total
Curto's Brigade: 13th Chasseurs, 22nd Chasseurs	39	863	902
Brigade ?: 3rd Hussars, 14th Chasseurs, 26th Chasseurs	42	857	899

BOYER'S DIVISION

	Officers	Men	Total
6th, 11th, 15th and 25th Dragoons	67	1,404	1,471
Total Cavalry	148	3,324	3,472

AUXILIARY TROOPS	Officers	Men	Total
Reserve Artillery One HA, 4 Field Batteries	11	379	390
1 Company Pontoniers, Train, Artificers etc.	10	763	773
Engineers: 2 Companies Sappers	5	190	195
Gendarmerie	5	169	174
Wagon Train, Mule Train etc.	35	898	933
Total Auxiliary Arms	66	2,389	2,455
TOTAL OF THE ARMY OF PORTUGAL	536	16,904	17,440
TOTAL NUMBER OF FRENCH TROOPS	2,032	67,745	69,767

ABOVE **Wellington's view of the battlefield from above the village of Villodas. From this vantage point Wellington, after he had ridden forward from Nanclares to join the Light Division, could see the whole of the immediate battlefield from the knoll of Iruna above Tres Puentes, to the bridge of Mendoza, to the knoll of Arinez - visible in the centre of this photo - and across to the heights of Puebla.**

LEFT **The bridge over the Zadorra at Puebla de Arganzon. It was here that Hill's column crossed the river prior to the battle. In the far distance the western end of the heights of Puebla can be seen.**

THE BATTLE OF VITTORIA

THE BATTLEFIELD

The last few days on the advance to Vittoria had been very cold. This, coupled with the rain which had fallen throughout 19 June, made it an unpleasant time for both armies. Later, however, Wellington's men would greet rain on the eve of battle as a good omen. On 20 June Wellington rode out from Subjiana de Morillas and carried out his usual reconnaissance of the field before him. Through the gloom and mist he marked down the French dispositions. The battlefield itself is long and rectangular, some 12 miles long and six miles wide. The great road to Bayonne cuts the centre of the valley, which is horseshoe-shaped, with the heights of Puebla hanging over the southern edge of the field and the Sierra de Badaya enclosing the western and northern boundaries. The river Zadorra, having cut its way through a gorge at the entrance to the valley at Puebla de Arganzon, meanders in a north-easterly direction as far as the village of Tres Puentes, where it straightens out and flows directly east, passing by Vittoria itself about two miles north of the town. In 1813 there were ten bridges across the Zadorra; remarkably none were blown up by the French, although the river is fordable in many places anyway. Dotted along the river, or close by it, are several villages, beginning at Nanclares in the west, then Villodas, Tres Puentes, Margarita, Crispiana, Gobeo, Yurre, Abechuco, Gamarra Mayor, Gamarra Minor and Durana. Along the foot of the heights of Puebla there are three small villages – from Subjiana de Alava in the west to Zumelzu, Esquivel and then Armentia. Along the great road through the centre of the battlefield are Arinez and Gomecha, while La Hermandad, Zuazo and Ali are found between the road and the Zadorra. The valley floor is undulating, and although there are some imposing slopes between Ali and Armentia, there is nothing that resembles the crest behind which Wellington placed his army at Waterloo. The one outstanding feature is the knoll of Arinez: a great, dominating, two-peaked hill which stands to the north of the great road in front of Arinez. At the 'open' end of the valley lies Vittoria itself, much smaller in 1813 than it is today, with the villages of Betono, Zurbano, Elorriaga and Ilarraza beyond it. Vittoria is a great centre of communications, with the great road to France running north-east out of the town, through Durana and on towards France, and the road to Salvatierra and Pamplona running east. The road to Bilbao runs north, and to the south-west runs the road to Logrono.

FRENCH DISPOSITIONS

Gazan's Army of the South held the first line in a position stretching from the knoll of Arinez to the village of Subjiana de Alava, with outposts covering the entrance to the valley at the gorge of Puebla de Arganzon. The second line consisted of two divisions of D'Erlon's Army of the Centre, which held a position on either side of the great road in front of the village of Gomecha. Both these lines faced west, in keeping with Joseph's conviction that the Allied attack would come from this direction. Joseph's Royal Guards, along with the majority of the French cavalry, were held in reserve to the west of Vittoria, probably around Zuazo. On 20 June Reille's Army of Portugal occupied a position on the slopes between Ali and Armentia, but before dawn on 21 June, having received information that Allied troops had been seen marching east, well to the north of the battlefield (this was Longa), Reille began moving his brigades north and deploying them along the Zadorra between Arriaga and Durana, to watch the pas-

BELOW **The view that both Joseph and Jourdan would have had from the western peak of the knoll of Arinez. The village on the right is Tres Puentes, whilst that on the left is Villodas. The two are separated by the knoll of Iruna. It was onto this piece of ground that Kempt's brigade managed to make his way unseen during the battle. The buildings immediately to the left of the knoll are part of a modern factory.**

RIGHT **The same position, but looking directly west from the knoll of Arinez. In the far distance is the village of Nanclares. Villodas is the village at right centre, separated from the modern factory by the Zadorra, the winding course of which is marked by the line of trees. Behind Villodas are the dips and folds which concealed the Light Division during the early stages of the battle.**

sage of the river. The villages of Abechuco and Gamarra Mayor, on the northern bank of the river, were also occupied. Thus the French line on 21 June formed an 'L' shape, with the angle being the village of Margarita. The French troops holding these positions numbered around 60,000, with 153 guns.

ALLIED DISPOSITIONS

Some 78,000 British, Spanish and Portuguese troops with 96 guns opposed the French, a force which Wellington planned to split into four columns in order to hit at key points along the French line. The right column, under Hill and consisting of the 2nd Division, Morillo's Spanish division and Silveira's Portuguese, supported by Victor Alten's and Fane's cavalry, was to pass the Zadorra at Puebla de Arganzon before storming the heights of Puebla and the villages along the foot of them, with Subjiana de Alava being the first. The troops atop the heights were to drive the French back along their entire length and in so doing turn the French left flank. The two centre columns, nominally under Wellington's personal command, totalled some 30,000 troops.

The first centre column consisted of the Light and 4th divisions and the cavalry brigades of Robert Hill, Grant and Ponsonby as well as D'Urban's Portuguese. It was to advance from Subjiana de Morillas as far as Nanclares, where it was to wait opposite the two bridges there until Hill's division had established itself on the heights of Puebla. It was then to cross the Zadorra and make a frontal attack on the French centre.

ABOVE **Wellington and his staff at the battle of Vittoria. In this marvellous painting by Beavis, a Spanish peasant, possibly Jose Ortiz de Zarate, passes on vital information to Wellington while British cavalry and artillery advance in front of them. The heights of Puebla can be seen in the background while the two peaks in the centre are, presumably, intended to be the knoll of Arinez, though greatly exaggerated.**

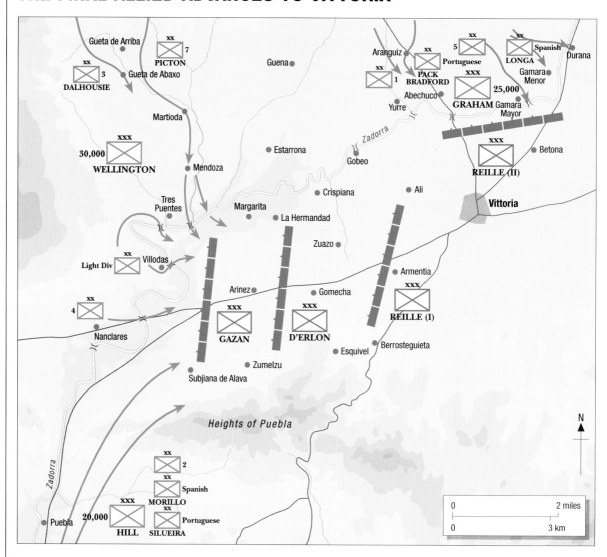

The other centre column consisted of the 3rd and 7th divisions and was under the command – somewhat controversially – of Lord Dalhousie, because Picton had irritated Wellington with his complaints during the advance. The column was to move east through the mountains to the north of the battlefield, using narrow tracks, before debouching onto the valley floor at the small villages of Las Guetas. From here the two divisions would be in a position to strike directly south and attack the rear of the French front line, approximately at the angle of the 'L'.

The final Allied column consisted of 20,000 troops under Graham – the 1st and 5th divisions, Longa's Spaniards and the Portuguese brigades of Pack and Bradford. These were supported by Anson's light dragoons and Bock's heavy dragoons. To Graham fell the most important task of all, namely the cutting of the great road to France. He was to march to the north of the mountains through which the 3rd and 7th divisions were moving and swing south to attack the right of the French

line. He was given a great deal of latitude by Wellington, whose instructions placed a great responsibility upon him. Graham was to cut the great road to France and, if all was going well elsewhere, to press hard and drive into the rear of the main French fighting line. However, he was not to press too hard, in case it drew so many French reinforcements upon him that his prime objective could not be achieved. As it turned out, Graham did exactly what his chief had asked of him, although, as we shall see, had he been a little more aggressive in his actions, he might have achieved much more.

In addition to the four columns there were 12,000 Spanish troops under Giron, who had made a wide sweep to the north of the main Allied army, at one point threatening Bilbao. Giron made a great effort to reach the battlefield but, like Craufurd at Talavera, was ultimately too late. The scene was set, therefore, with Wellington having staked all on the synchronisation of four attacking columns scattered over a distance of ten miles. On the French side, Joseph and Jourdan, the latter having just recovered from a bout of fever, were confident in their ability and hoped that Clausel and the Army of the North would arrive in time to play a part in the fighting.

ABOVE **A dramatic view of the western half of the battlefield of Vittoria, as seen from the heights of Puebla. The village in the centre at the foot of the heights is Subjiana de Alava with the main road running east-west clearly discernible. To the north of the road, on the left of the picture, is the wooded area which hid the Light Division prior to the battle. The village to the right of this area is Villodas and Tres Puentes is just visible beyond that. The knoll of Arinez is on the right of the picture to the north of the road with the village of Arinez itself on the extreme right edge of the photo. In the distance can be seen the low range of hills from where Picton and Dalhousie debouched (not the hills beyond on the skyline).**

THE BATTLE BEGINS

The timings of the actions throughout this chapter are all approximate, and are my own judgement, based upon the sequence of events; French and British accounts differ, dramatically in some cases. There is nothing like the clear-cut timings of the sequence of events at Waterloo, for example.

ABOVE **A view from the low ridge south of Arinez looking towards the village of Subjiana de Alava, with the heights of Puebla in the background. The village was attacked by O'Callaghan's brigade of the 2nd Division and was the scene of fierce, if somewhat brief, fighting. O'Callaghan's brigade later advanced across these fields from right to left under enemy artillery fire.**

The battle of Vittoria began at about 8.00am on 21 June 1813. The gloom and rain of the preceding days had given way to a clear, crisp morning, but the peace and tranquillity were soon shattered by the noise of battle as the two sides began what was to prove the decisive battle of the Peninsular War. The first Allied troops into action were those of Hill's 2nd Division, who, supported by Morillo's Spaniards, climbed the western end of the heights of Puebla to begin the attack. Leading the way were the 1/71st, 1/50th and the 1/92nd, belonging to Cadogan's brigade, but these were soon passed on their right by Morillo's Spaniards, whose task it was to clear the French voltigeurs from a spur which overlooked the road and commanded not only the entrance to the valley of the Zadorra but the western end of the heights of Puebla themselves. Morillo's men succeeded in clearing the way, advancing over the rocky, scrub-covered hillside, and driving the French back until they were halted by Maransin's brigade, consisting of the 12th Leger and 45th Line, which Gazan had sent up from the left of the main French line around Subjiana de Alava. The fight quickly developed into a sharp contest as Cadogan's regiment, the 71st, and the light companies of Cadogan and Byng's brigades entered the fray. Morillo himself was badly wounded, but the French were thrown back and the western end of the heights remained secure in Allied hands. The 50th and 92nd were brought forward to consolidate this important position.

After just an hour or so the French position had already been compromised, for if Hill continued to drive along the summit of the heights of Puebla, he would succeed in turning the French left flank. This danger was not lost on the French, however, and before long the 32nd Line and 43rd Line were climbing onto the heights to try and stop the Allies, while St Pol's brigade – the 21st Leger and 100th Line – was sent in to plug the gap left by Maransin's brigade. The fight on the summit flared up with great intensity, but the Allied troops clung to their lofty position, driving the French back, but only after Cadogan himself had been mortally wounded. His men propped him up against a couple of knapsacks in order that he could watch the progress of the battle. Meanwhile, his

brigade pushed forward with Morillo's Spaniards, while O'Callaghan's brigade, consisting of the 1/28th, 1/34th and 1/39th and one company of the 5/60th, advanced along the slopes beneath them and along the valley floor against the small village of Subjiana de Alava, which was defended by St Pol's two regiments of Daricau's division. The fight here developed quickly as O'Callaghan's men attacked over the bare lower slopes of the heights of Puebla. They entered the village, but were unable to debouch owing to artillery fire from the divisional battery of Conroux's division and a determined counter-attack by the 55th and 58th of Schwitter's brigade. The 1/28th and 1/39th, after attempting to advance from Subjiana, were forced to retreat to the cover of the village. Here, the fighting escalated, as the French attempted to drive O'Callaghan's men out. They were unsuccessful, however, and once again the British troops tried to advance east from the village, only to be driven back yet again by Schwitter's brigade and by the 32nd and 43rd of Rey's former brigade. (Rey had left on 19 June to escort part of the convoy.) The situation developed into a stalemate, with the British unable to debouch from the village and the French unable to recapture it.

ABOVE **A view of the summit of the heights of Puebla, looking west from a position above Zumelzu. Morillo's Spanish division and Cadogan's brigade fought their way along the top, advancing towards the camera. The peak in the centre marks the gorge at the entrance to the valley of the Zadorra.**

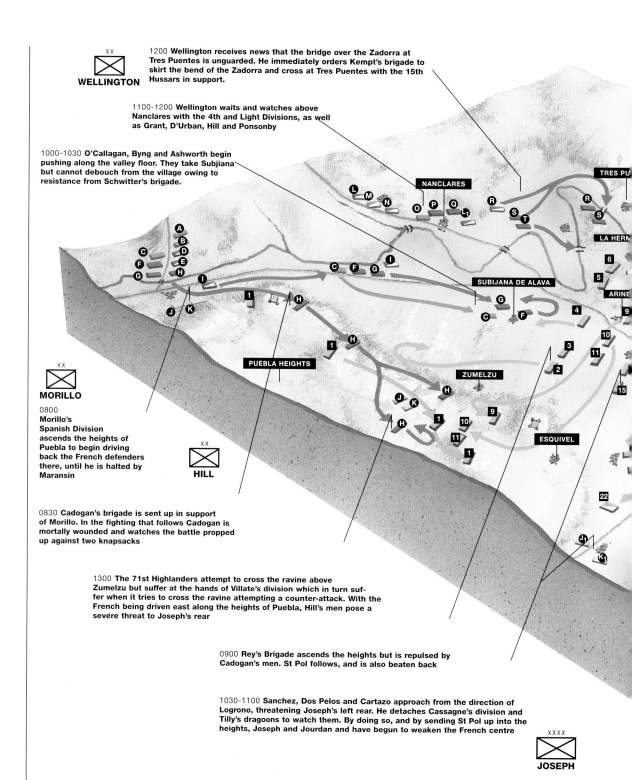

1200 Wellington receives news that the bridge over the Zadorra at Tres Puentes is unguarded. He immediately orders Kempt's brigade to skirt the bend of the Zadorra and cross at Tres Puentes with the 15th Hussars in support.

1100-1200 Wellington waits and watches above Nanclares with the 4th and Light Divisions, as well as Grant, D'Urban, Hill and Ponsonby

1000-1030 O'Callagan, Byng and Ashworth begin pushing along the valley floor. They take Subjiana but cannot debouch from the village owing to resistance from Schwitter's brigade.

WELLINGTON

NANCLARES

TRES PU

LA HERM

SUBIJANA DE ALAVA

PUEBLA HEIGHTS

ZUMELZU

ARINE

ESQUIVEL

MORILLO

0800 Morillo's Spanish Division ascends the heights of Puebla to begin driving back the French defenders there, until he is halted by Maransin

HILL

0830 Cadogan's brigade is sent up in support of Morillo. In the fighting that follows Cadogan is mortally wounded and watches the battle propped up against two knapsacks

1300 The 71st Highlanders attempt to cross the ravine above Zumelzu but suffer at the hands of Villate's division which in turn suffer when it tries to cross the ravine attempting a counter-attack. With the French being driven east along the heights of Puebla, Hill's men pose a sévère threat to Joseph's rear

0900 Rey's Brigade ascends the heights but is repulsed by Cadogan's men. St Pol follows, and is also beaten back

1030-1100 Sanchez, Dos Pelos and Cartazo approach from the direction of Logrono, threatening Joseph's left rear. He detaches Cassagne's division and Tilly's dragoons to watch them. By doing so, and by sending St Pol up into the heights, Joseph and Jourdan and have begun to weaken the French centre

JOSEPH

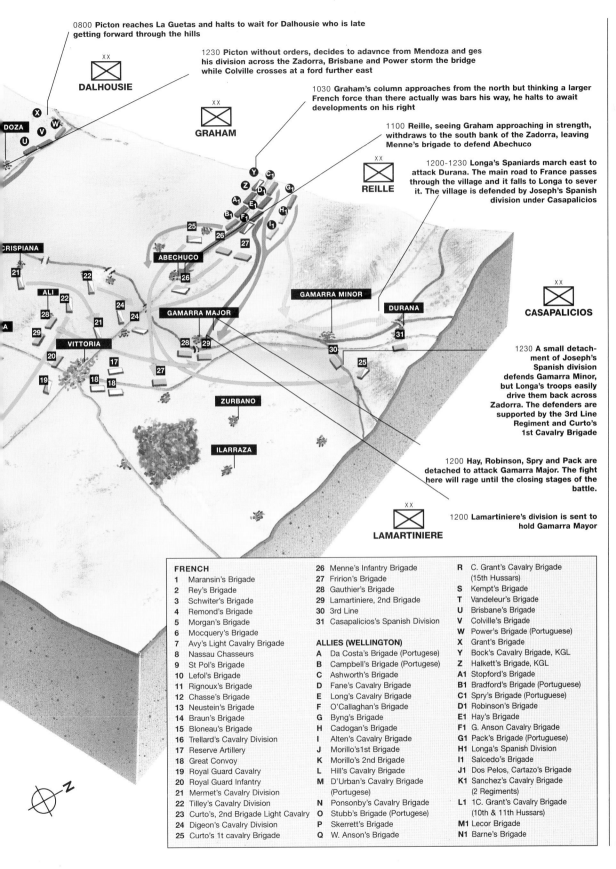

0800 Picton reaches La Guetas and halts to wait for Dalhousie who is late getting forward through the hills

DALHOUSIE XX

1230 Picton without orders, decides to adavnce from Mendoza and ges his division across the Zadorra, Brisbane and Power storm the bridge while Colville crosses at a ford further east

DOZA

GRAHAM XX

1030 Graham's column approaches from the north but thinking a larger French force than there actually was bars his way, he halts to await developments on his right

1100 Reille, seeing Graham approaching in strength, withdraws to the south bank of the Zadorra, leaving Menne's brigade to defend Abechuco

REILLE XX

1200-1230 Longa's Spaniards march east to attack Durana. The main road to France passes through the village and it falls to Longa to sever it. The village is defended by Joseph's Spanish division under Casapalicios

25
26
27

ABECHUCO

CRISPIANA

21

26

ALI
22
22
28
21
24
24

29

GAMARRA MAJOR

GAMARRA MINOR

DURANA

CASAPALICIOS XX

VITTORIA
20
17
19
18
18

28
29
27
31

30
25

1230 A small detachment of Joseph's Spanish division defends Gamarra Minor, but Longa's troops easily drive them back across Zadorra. The defenders are supported by the 3rd Line Regiment and Curto's 1st Cavalry Brigade

ZURBANO

ILARRAZA

1200 Hay, Robinson, Spry and Pack are detached to attack Gamarra Major. The fight here will rage until the closing stages of the battle.

LAMARTINIERE XX

1200 Lamartiniere's division is sent to hold Gamarra Mayor

N

FRENCH		
1	Maransin's Brigade	
2	Rey's Brigade	
3	Schwiter's Brigade	
4	Remond's Brigade	
5	Morgan's Brigade	
6	Mocquery's Brigade	
7	Avy's Light Cavalry Brigade	
8	Nassau Chasseurs	
9	St Pol's Brigade	
10	Lefol's Brigade	
11	Rignoux's Brigade	
12	Chasse's Brigade	
13	Neustein's Brigade	
14	Braun's Brigade	
15	Bloneau's Brigade	
16	Trellard's Cavalry Division	
17	Reserve Artillery	
18	Great Convoy	
19	Royal Guard Cavalry	
20	Royal Guard Infantry	
21	Mermet's Cavalry Division	
22	Tilley's Cavalry Division	
23	Curto's, 2nd Brigade Light Cavalry	
24	Digeon's Cavalry Division	
25	Curto's 1t cavalry Brigade	

26	Menne's Infantry Brigade
27	Fririon's Brigade
28	Gauthier's Brigade
29	Lamartiniere, 2nd Brigade
30	3rd Line
31	Casapalicios's Spanish Division

ALLIES (WELLINGTON)

A	Da Costa's Brigade (Portugese)
B	Campbell's Brigade (Portugese)
C	Ashworth's Brigade
D	Fane's Cavalry Brigade
E	Long's Cavalry Brigade
F	O'Callaghan's Brigade
G	Byng's Brigade
H	Cadogan's Brigade
I	Alten's Cavalry Brigade
J	Morillo's1st Brigade
K	Morillo's 2nd Brigade
L	Hill's Cavalry Brigade
M	D'Urban's Cavalry Brigade (Portugese)
N	Ponsonby's Cavalry Brigade
O	Stubb's Brigade (Portugese)
P	Skerrett's Brigade
Q	W. Anson's Brigade

R	C. Grant's Cavalry Brigade (15th Hussars)
S	Kempt's Brigade
T	Vandeleur's Brigade
U	Brisbane's Brigade
V	Colville's Brigade
W	Power's Brigade (Portuguese)
X	Grant's Brigade
Y	Bock's Cavalry Brigade, KGL
Z	Halkett's Brigade, KGL
A1	Stopford's Brigade
B1	Bradford's Brigade (Portuguese)
C1	Spry's Brigade (Portuguese)
D1	Robinson's Brigade
E1	Hay's Brigade
F1	G. Anson Cavalry Brigade
G1	Pack's Brigade (Portuguese)
H1	Longa's Spanish Division
I1	Salcedo's Brigade
J1	Dos Pelos, Cartazo's Brigade
K1	Sanchez's Cavalry Brigade (2 Regiments)
L1	1C. Grant's Cavalry Brigade (10th & 11th Hussars)
M1	Lecor Brigade
N1	Barne's Brigade

RIGHT **Kempt's view of the knoll of Arinez, looking south from his position on the knoll of Iruna above Tres Puentes. The knoll is, in fact, two separate hills (centre and right). The two dark humps in the left background are the hills below Gomecha.**

BELOW **The 15th Hussars cross the bridge at Tres Puentes in support of Kempt's brigade of the Light Division. Caton Woodville's picture shows the bridge as being just a fraction of its real length. Otherwise it is fairly accurate with Kempt's infantry formed up on the knoll of Iruna and the knoll of Arinez in the background.**

RIGHT **The bridge over the Zadorra at Villodas, with the village in the background. Some of Leval's skirmishers crossed this bridge early in the day and engaged Allied troops in the village before being thrown back. Vandeleur's brigade of the Light Division crossed this bridge during the afternoon.**

While Hill's men were driving forward along the summit of the heights of Puebla, the Allied columns under Picton and Graham – Dalhousie had been delayed – had become clearly visible to Joseph and Jourdan as the Allied troops emerged from the heights to the north of the Zadorra. Jourdan, convinced that the Allied columns to the north of the Zadorra were merely for show, firmly believed that Hill's attack posed the greatest threat to him, so he began to weaken his centre in order to stem the advance of the Allies along the heights of Puebla. Villatte's division, waiting patiently in reserve in front of Gomecha, was ordered to march via Esquivel up onto the summit of the heights to block Hill's advance, while Tilly's dragoons moved from their position on the Logrono road, close to Berostigueta, to the south, to check whether there were further Allied columns moving east to the south of the heights of Puebla. Jordan even sent two infantry divisions from Gomecha to support Tilly, such was his paranoia. The effect of this was to begin the crucial weakening of his centre, which is just what Wellington had hoped for. Indeed, to compound his error, Jourdan ordered Conroux's division to move against O'Callaghan's brigade in Subjiana, supported by both Maransin and St Pol's brigades, who were then to join Villatte in driving the Allies from the heights of Puebla. The result of all this was that just two of Hill's brigades – O'Callaghan's and Cadogan's – and one Spanish division had drawn off two whole French divisions as well as the brigades of Maransin and St Pol. So far, things were going well for Wellington in this sector.

Elsewhere, however, it was a different story. Wellington had been watching from his vantage point on the knoll above Nanclares with growing impatience for signs of the flanking columns of Dalhousie and Graham. Yet 11.00am came and went and still there was no sign of them. Nor were there any audible sounds from the east to indicate that Graham had entered the fight.

The French troops confronting Graham belonged to Reille's Army of Portugal and consisted of Sarrut's division and Curto's light cavalry brigade. They were positioned near the village of Aranguiz. In support of these troops were Lamartiniere's division and the dragoons of Boyer and Digeon, all in positions on the south bank of the Zadorra. Meanwhile, Graham, having marched south from Olano, halted and, following the instructions given him by Wellington, waited to see how matters were faring away to his right. Having been told not to be drawn into any heavy fighting, Graham watched and waited; he had seen the strength of the French force in front of him. Reille, on the other hand, saw that the Allied force bearing down upon him was also of great

LEFT **The bridge over the Zadorra at Tres Puentes. Kempt's brigade of the Light Division crossed from left to right on to the knoll of Iruna. The height from which this picture was taken shielded Kempt from the enemy's view and allowed him to cross relatively easily.**

strength and he decided not to dispute any ground to the north of the Zadorra. Instead he withdrew his troops to the villages of Gamarra Mayor, Gamarra Minor and Abechuco, on the northern bank of the river; Graham would need to take these villages if he were to engage the French armies south of the river and join in the main Allied attack.

It was about noon when Reille, having seen Graham send forward Pack's Portuguese brigade and Longa's Spanish division against the village of Aranguiz, pulled back his men to the three villages. This allowed Graham to deploy his column for a full frontal attack, and he duly sent Longa eastwards to attack Gamarra Minor and Durana, the latter village marking the extreme right of the French position. Durana was of great importance because the great road to Bayonne ran through it. Once this village was taken the first of Graham's two tasks would have been accomplished. Gamarra Mayor, meanwhile, was to be attacked by the 5th Division under John Oswald, who commanded the

ABOVE **The bridge over the Zadorra, used by D'Urban's Portuguese cavalry who crossed from left to right.**

division in the absence of the usual commander, Sir James Leith. Further west the 1st Division and the Portuguese brigades of Spry and Bradford deployed in front of Abechuco.

Longa's Spaniards took Gamarra Minor without too great a struggle and then continued east along the Zadorra as far as Durana, which was defended by a Spanish division in French service, under Casapalicios. The fight for Durana was far more fierce than that for Gamarra Minor, and it was not until the early afternoon that Longa actually fought his way to the narrow bridge over the Zadorra, though he was unable to force his way across it and enter the village. It was here at Durana that the Allies fought for one of the main objectives of the battle – the cutting of the great road to Bayonne and with it Joseph's communications with France. It is a curious commentary on the fight at Durana that such an important and key village, having the main road to Bayonne run through it, should have been fought over by troops who might be considered 'secondary' – i.e. Spanish troops. This is not meant in any derogatory sense but one might have expected Reille to have

THE FIGHTING AT GAMARRA MAYOR

Some of the hardest fighting of 21 June 1813 took place in the small village of Gamarra Mayor, an important post on the French right flank. It was one of the vital river crossings over the Zadorra and was defended by men from Reille's Army of Portugal, men who according to one British soldier, 'appear to have formed a determination not to be beat.' This painting shows the 5th Division in action in the streets of Gamarra Mayor with units form Robinson's brigade, the 1/4th and 2/59th, intermixed with each other, engaging in close-quarter fighting with the French 118th and 119th regiments. Although the Allies were able to thrust the defenders from the village they were unable to debouch from the place as French artillery swept all exits as well as the long, narrow bridge across the Zadorra. This painting closely follows the famous painting by Beadle, featured elsewhere in this book. Sadly, the painting today lies in poor condition in the bowels of a Leicestershire Museum. (Bill Younghusband)

left the defence of such a key position to French troops. Indeed, the decision to send Maucune back to France on mere escort duty on the morning of the battle was turning out to be a bad one, for his men would have been of great use at Durana.

At Gamarra Mayor, meanwhile, the fighting was turning particularly bloody. The small village was defended by two regiments of Gauthier's brigade – the 118th and 119th – who had barricaded the long bridge over the Zadorra and the streets around it. The British troops given the task of driving the French out belonged to Robinson's brigade of the 5th Division, the 1/4th, 2/47th and the 2/59th. The first troops to gain a foothold in the village were the 1/4th. They drove the French steadily back amid heavy fighting in the streets and around the church. The defenders were forced from the village, abandoning three guns but, as at Durana, the French had covered the exits and the bridge itself with guns and each attempt to debouch from the village ended in bloody failure. Here the fight reached stalemate, and as the piles of British bodies around the bridge began to grow, Robinson ordered his men to halt and wait for artillery support.

It was around noon, and there was still no sign of the centre columns under Dalhousie and Picton. Graham, whose orders dictated that much of his own actions were to be based upon the movements of these two columns on his right, continued his attacks regardless. Wellington, meanwhile, grew more apprehensive. The synchronisation of such a large-scale flanking movement was difficult at best. If all worked well, the results could be devastating for the French. However, if things went the other way they might prove disastrous for Wellington. As the sounds of musketry and artillery fire echoed along the valley of the Zadorra from the direction of Graham's attack, Wellington must have watched and waited with a sense of anxiety.

At 11.30 Wellington rode forward from his position on the knoll above Nanclares to join the Light Division which was hidden from enemy view in the dips and folds in the ground between Nanclares and Villodas. In Villodas there had been some skirmishing between the light infantry of the French 9th Leger and the riflemen of the 2/95th. The

latter drove the French back across the bridge and onto the right bank of the Zadorra, upon which Wellington rode forward to the hill above the village. Wellington continued to observe the battle unfold from his position on the hill behind Villodas. This affords a wonderful panoramic view of the battlefield from Mendoza, across to the knoll of Arinez and up on to the heights of Puebla. Some time around noon, while Wellington watched the progress of the battle with his staff, a 53-year-old Spanish peasant named Jose Ortiz de Zarate appeared and told him that the bridge over the Zadorra at Tres Puentes had been left unguarded by the French. This startling piece of information was digested by Wellington with great relish. Quick to seize upon such an opportunity, he ordered Kempt's brigade of the Light Division, consisting of the 1/95th, 3/95th and the 1/43rd, to march around the great hairpin bend of the river and cross as quickly as possible. The bend of the river took the form of a great overhanging height which shielded the bridge from prying French eyes, although it has to be said that Joseph's men were guilty of great neglect by not guarding the bridge. Once

BELOW **The French 118th Regiment at Vittoria. This regiment was one of the French units which defended the village of Gamarra Mayor against the 5th Division and was responsible for barring the way across the Zadorra until very late in the day. Indeed, the fighting at Gamarra Mayor was probably the bloodiest anywhere on the battlefield.**

Kempt's men had crossed the bridge, they began deploying on top of the height overlooking the bridge from where they could see before them the French troops occupying the right hand end of Leval's line. Unfortunately, the Spanish peasant, Zarate, was not among them, having been decapitated by one of only two shots to be fired at Kempt's brigade by the French. The 15th Hussars crossed the bridge shortly afterwards and there followed an anxious wait as the British troops prepared to face the French counter-attack, which they assumed would not be long in coming. However, things were to prove quite different, for just as they began to take up positions to face a French advance, they saw the French begin to pull back.

The hasty withdrawal of the French was caused by the appearance of Picton's 3rd Division opposite the bridge of Mendoza. Picton's division had begun to debouch from the hills around Las Guetas at around midday, but Lord Dalhousie, commanding the 7th Division and the two columns of Wellington's left centre, refused to allow Picton's division, which was in front, to advance further than the village of Mendoza. Apparently Dalhousie was worried by the fact that two of his brigades, those of Barnes and Le Cor, had been delayed in the mountains and had still to come up with the rest of the 7th Division, Le Cor's Portuguese. Also, Dalhousie, like Graham, had orders to regulate his movements by events on his flank which, in Dalhousie's case, meant his left flank. Graham had yet to fully engage his force and so Dalhousie chose to stop and wait for orders.

VITTORIA: PHASE II 1330-1800

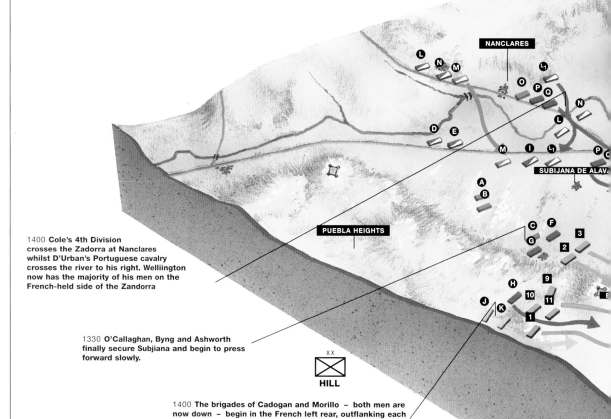

XX
WELLINGTON

NANCLARES

SUBIJANA DE ALAV.

PUEBLA HEIGHTS

1400 **Cole's 4th Division** crosses the Zadorra at Nanclares whilst D'Urban's Portuguese cavalry crosses the river to his right. Welliington now has the majority of his men on the French-held side of the Zandorra

1330 **O'Callaghan, Byng and Ashworth** finally secure Subjiana and begin to press forward slowly.

XX
HILL

1400 **The brigades of Cadogan and Morillo** – both men are now down – begin in the French left rear, outflanking each subsequent French position.

XX
GAZAN

FRENCH		
1	Maransin's Brigade	
2	Rey's Brigade	
3	Schwiter's Brigade	
4	Remond's Brigade	
5	Morgan's Brigade	
6	Mocquery's Brigade	
7	Avy's Light Cavalry Brigade	
8	Nassau Chasseurs	
9	St Pol's Brigade	
10	Lefol's Brigade	
11	Rignoux's Brigade	
12	Chasse's Brigade	
13	Neustein's Brigade	
14	Braun's Brigade	
15	Bloneau's Brigade	
16	Trellard's Cavalry Division	
17	Reserve Artillery	
18	Great Convoy	
19	Royal Guard Cavalry	
20	Royal Guard Infantry	
21	Mermet's Cavalry Division	
22	Tilley's Cavalry Division	
23	Curto's, 2nd Brigade Light Cavalry	
24	Digeon's Cavalry Division	
25	Curto's 1t cavalry Brigade	

26	Menne's Infantry Brigade
27	Fririon's Brigade
28	Gauthier's Brigade
29	Lamartiniere, 2nd Brigade
30	3rd Line
31	Casapalicios's Spanish Division

ALLIES (WELLINGTON)

A	Da Costa's Brigade (Portugese)
B	Campbell's Brigade (Portugese)
C	Ashworth's Brigade
D	Fane's Cavalry Brigade
E	Long's Cavalry Brigade
F	O'Callaghan's Brigade
G	Byng's Brigade
H	Cadogan's Brigade
I	Alten's Cavalry Brigade
J	Morillo's1st Brigade
K	Morillo's 2nd Brigade
L	Hill's Cavalry Division
M	D'Urban's Cavalry Brigade (Portugese)
N	Ponsonby's Cavalry Brigade
O	Stubb's Brigade (Portugese)
P	Skerrett's Brigade
Q	W. Anson's Brigade

R	C. Grant's Cavalry Brigade (15th Hussars)
S	Kempt's Brigade
T	Vandeleur's Brigade
U	Brisbane's Brigade
V	Colville's Brigade
W	Power's Brigade (Portuguese)
X	Grant's Brigade
Y	Bock's Cavalry Brigade, KGL
Z	Halkett's Brigade, KGL
A1	Stopford's Brigade
B1	Bradford's Brigade (Portuguese)
C1	Spry's Brigade (Portuguese)
D1	Robinson's Brigade
E1	Hay's Brigade
F1	G. Anson Cavalry Brigade
G1	Pack's Brigade (Portuguese)
H1	Longa's Spanish Division
I1	Salcedo's Brigade
J1	Dos Pelos, Cartazo's Brigade
K1	Sanchez's Cavalry Brigade (2 Regiments)
L1	1C. Grant's Cavalry Brigade (10th & 11th Hussars)
M1	Lecor Brigade
N1	Barne's Brigade

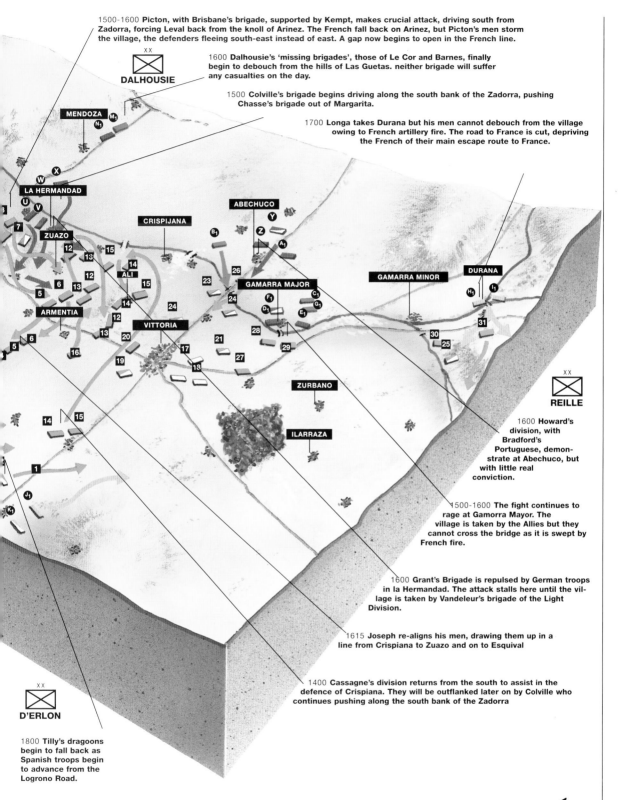

1500-1600 Picton, with Brisbane's brigade, supported by Kempt, makes crucial attack, driving south from Zadorra, forcing Leval back from the knoll of Arinez. The French fall back on Arinez, but Picton's men storm the village, the defenders fleeing south-east instead of east. A gap now begins to open in the French line.

1600 Dalhousie's 'missing brigades', those of Le Cor and Barnes, finally begin to debouch from the hills of Las Guetas. neither brigade will suffer any casualties on the day.

1500 Colville's brigade begins driving along the south bank of the Zadorra, pushing Chasse's brigade out of Margarita.

1700 Longa takes Durana but his men cannot debouch from the village owing to French artillery fire. The road to France is cut, depriving the French of their main escape route to France.

DALHOUSIE

MENDOZA

LA HERMANDAD

CRISPIJANA

ABECHUCO

ZUAZO

ALI

VITTORIA

GAMARRA MAJOR

GAMARRA MINOR

DURANA

ARMENTIA

ZURBANO

ILARRAZA

REILLE

1600 Howard's division, with Bradford's Portuguese, demonstrate at Abechuco, but with little real conviction.

1500-1600 The fight continues to rage at Gamorra Mayor. The village is taken by the Allies but they cannot cross the bridge as it is swept by French fire.

1600 Grant's Brigade is repulsed by German troops in la Hermandad. The attack stalls here until the village is taken by Vandeleur's brigade of the Light Division.

1615 Joseph re-aligns his men, drawing them up in a line from Crispiana to Zuazo and on to Esquival

1400 Cassagne's division returns from the south to assist in the defence of Crispiana. They will be outflanked later on by Colville who continues pushing along the south bank of the Zadorra

D'ERLON

1800 Tilly's dragoons begin to fall back as Spanish troops begin to advance from the Logrono Road.

N

51

Meanwhile, Picton, the fiery Welshman, sat on his horse waiting for orders. The ensuing story is well known but is worth repeating for it gives us a wonderful portrait of Picton and his own inimitable approach to warfare. Apparently, Picton grew more and more impatient for orders as the early afternoon wore on, the more so since he could plainly see events unfolding on the heights of Puebla, away to the south. At length, an aide arrived and, riding up to Picton, enquired as to the whereabouts of Lord Dalhousie. An exasperated Picton replied that he did not know, and he asked the aide whether there were any orders for him. "None," replied the aide, at which an increasingly angry Picton cried, "Then pray, sir, what are the orders you do bring?" "Why, that as soon as Lord Dalhousie, with the seventh division, shall commence an attack upon that bridge," said the aide, pointing to the bridge of Mendoza, "the Fourth and Light are to support him." Picton was astonished by the statement and could not conceive of the idea of any other division fighting in front of his own. After all, the 3rd Division was not called the 'fighting' division for nothing. Drawing himself up in his saddle, Picton growled at the aide-de-camp and said simply, "You may tell Lord Wellington from me, sir, that the Third Division, under my command, shall in less than ten minutes attack the bridge and carry it, and the Fourth and Light divisions may support if they choose." Turning to his men, he shouted, "Come on, ye rascals! Come on ye fighting villains!" and led them off to attack the bridge. It was to be one of the turning points of the battle.

Unlike the bridges at Gamarra Mayor and Durana, which were heavily defended and swept by French guns, the bridge over the Zadorra was relatively unguarded, save for 500 of Avy's cavalry and three guns. These were no match for Picton's veterans, and soon the 3rd Division was bearing down upon the bridge with Brisbane's brigade leading and Colville's heading for a ford about 300 yards to the east. The passage of the river was far from easy, however, with the mounted chasseurs of the 27th Regiment, the 28th Line and 2nd Nassauers under Darmagnac disputing the way. These were supported by German artillery, and it was only when Picton brought forward Captain Douglas's brigade of artillery that Brisbane's men, the 1/45th, 74th and 1/88th with three companies of the 5/60th, were able to sweep across the bridge, while Kempt's riflemen advanced from their knoll to help drive away both the cavalry and artillery. With Brisbane, Colville and Kempt safely across the Zadorra, followed by Power's Portuguese brigade, Wellington had established a crucial foothold on the French-held side of the river. Soon afterwards Cole's 4th Division crossed the Zadorra at Nanclares, and Vandeleur's brigade of the Light Division crossed at Villodas. The noose was beginning to tighten around Joseph's neck.

BELOW **A view of the knoll of Arinez looking south-west from the ground between Margarita and La Hermandad. Brisbane's brigade of the 3rd Division, supported by Kempt, swept past the knoll from right to left to attack Arinez itself. Their attack was to be one of the decisive moments of the battle.**

The first obvious French casualty was sure to be Leval unless he pulled back from his position in front of the knoll of Arinez, for his right flank hung limply in the air. Picton, riding at the head of Brisbane's brigade with Kempt in support, drove on behind the knoll, while Colville, supported by Grant's brigade of the 7th Division (which had finally arrived), advanced on Picton's left. Leval was left with little choice but to withdraw over the knoll into Arinez itself and onto the rising ground behind it. On the left of Leval and to the south of the main road to Vittoria were Schwitter's brigade from Conroux's division and Remond's brigade from Daricau's division. Once Leval had retired, they were forced to make a similar retrograde movement. As a consequence, the other two brigades of these divisions – that formerly under the command of Rey and that of St Pol – had to disengage from the fight around Subjiana de Alava, leaving O'Callaghan's brigade, the 50th and the 92nd free to continue their drive east along the valley floor and the lower slopes of the heights of Puebla.

These moves forced Jourdan and Joseph to take up a new position, which extended from Margarita, south to Gomecha and on to Zumelzu, with the village of Arinez held as a sort of forward position. The gap between Arinez and Margarita was filled by Darmagnac's division from the Army of the Centre. This new position extended for some two miles and was taken up in some confusion owing to the fact that several French units had to disengage the Allies in order to fall back. Indeed, so close were some of the Allied troops that they pursued the French all the way to the new position and, in effect, prevented them from settling into an effective order. The problem was that no matter where Jourdan re-aligned his men, he could not stop his line from being outflanked on its left by Hill's troops fighting their way along the heights of Puebla.

On the heights themselves, Villatte's division, which had been ordered to ascend and block Hill's advance, reached the summit at about 1.00pm and deployed, breathless after the climb across the narrow crest. Opposite them Morillo's Spaniards and the 71st Regiment, equally breathless, were ordered forward to keep the pressure on the French. They had reached a ravine – a geological fault – which impeded their advance and forced them to climb down a quite precipitous slope. They formed at the bottom of the fault with the Spaniards on the right and the 71st on their left, and together they began to climb the steep hillside opposite. One can only marvel at how they managed to scramble their way down to the bottom, let alone make the ascent on the other side. As the 71st advanced they noticed that the troops in front were

PICTON AND THE
3RD DIVISION STORM
THE BRIDGE OF MENDOZA
Picton had been waiting impatiently at Mendoza for orders as the early afternoon wore on. He could plainly see events unfolding on the heights of Puebla away to the south until at length, an aide arrived with orders for Lord Dalhousie to attack the bridge with the 4th and Light Divisions in support. The exasperated Picton was horrified and, drawing himself up in his saddle, growled at the astonished aide-de-camp

and said simply, 'You may tell Lord Wellington from me, sir, that the Third division under my command shall in less than ten minutes attack the bridge and carry it, and the Fourth and Light divisions may support if they choose.' Then, turning to his men, he shouted, 'Come on, ye rascals! Come on ye fighting villains!' before leading them off to attack the bridge. It was one of the turning points of the battle.

wearing light coloured greatcoats and white shako covers, and assumed, incorrectly, that these were Spaniards. Unfortunately, they were French troops, and as the Scots advanced, they were hit in front and flank by a withering fire that dropped at least 200 men in just a few seconds. The French advanced to follow up this success and took some 40 prisoners. Shortly afterwards, however, the tables were turned as Villatte, in an effort to consolidate his position, began to advance, his men climbing the Allied side of the fault where the 71st waited for them. Two volleys were enough to stop the French advance, and when the 50th and 92nd – who had been fighting their way along the lower slopes of the heights – came up at a charge, the French were thrown back in disorder. Two

LEFT **The sun shines on the grassy slope where the 71st came to grief on the heights of Puebla. The slope marks the far side of the ravine over which the 71st advanced, only to be met by a withering fire from the French who appeared at the top and on the right of the slope, their fire taking the 71st in both front and rear. Some 200 of their number were brought down here. The same fate awaited Villatte's troops when they attempted to attack over the same ground afterwards, attacking towards the camera.**

further French attacks here met with the same result. Shortly afterwards, Villatte withdrew the remains of his division, having received Jourdan's order to fall back to the new line. This effectively signalled an end to the serious fighting on the heights of Puebla, for whenever the Allied troops – now led by Cameron of the 92nd – came up against the French, the latter were pushed back with relative ease.

Back in the valley of the Zadorra, meanwhile, the Allies were beginning to pressure the new French position. The extreme right of the position was marked by the small village of Margarita, which was held by Chasse's brigade of Darmagnac's division. The village was attacked just before 3.00pm by Colville's brigade of the 3rd Division which, after crossing the ford over the Zadorra, had formed up and turned to its left to make its attack. The fighting was heavy for a time and it took Colville's men about half an hour to drive the defenders out, though the real reason for Chasse's withdrawal was the fact that his left had been exposed when Leval had pulled back to Arinez in the face of Picton's attack.

ABOVE **The bridge over the Zadorra at Durana. It was here that Spaniard fought Spaniard when Longa's Spanish division engaged in a fierce fight with Casapalicios's Spanish troops who were defending the bridge. It was here that one of the main Allied objectives was achieved, namely the cutting of the great road to France. It was accomplished during the late afternoon, thus depriving the French of their main escape route.**

A DECISIVE BLOW

Striking out diagonally after crossing the Zadorra, Picton moved around the base of the knoll of Arinez on its eastern side and launched an attack on the village of Arinez. Picton's formation comprised Power's Portuguese on the left and Brisbane's brigade on the right. These were supported by Kempt's brigade of the Light Division which, after seeing Brisbane cross the bridge of Mendoza, had come forward from the knoll above Tres Puentes and taken up a position behind Brisbane, sending out some companies of the 1/95th to clear the way. The riflemen, struck the village of Arinez first, working their way into the streets and to the church, where they began to fire upon the defenders. However, they were too few in number and were thrown out of the village soon afterwards by a French battalion. As the green-jacketed riflemen fell back, Brisbane brought his brigade forward, the fearsome 88th and the

74th leading the way. The ground around Arinez is undulating and space is tight owing to the close proximity of the knoll of Arinez itself, which dominates the area. Nonetheless, the 88th swept round to the south of the village and on to the main road while the 74th hit the village head on, with Power's Portuguese brigade attacking on their left. The 88th deployed from column into line, and as they approached the village, they were met by what one eye-witness described as a 'running fire' from right to left. The French defenders dropped scores of the Connaught Rangers but, undeterred, the 88th pressed on until they were within about 50 yards of the French firing line whereupon they shouldered arms and delivered their own devastating response. The French were severely shaken, and before they could reload for a second volley, they found themselves facing hundreds of cheering, red-jacketed soldiers, who emerged from the smoke with levelled bayonets. The French broke almost immediately and made off towards the village of Gomecha some

LEFT **The battle of Vittoria, after a drawing by Heath. Wellington, with obligatory telescope in hand, directs the attack by the 4th Division in the centre while a priest administers the last rites to a dying soldier, right.**

distance south-east of Arinez. Meanwhile, the 74th attacking Arinez on the left of the 88th swept into the village and sent the defenders fleeing onto the low rise behind; this position quickly became untenable too as the 88th swept along the main road, outflanking it to the south. The other battalion of Brisbane's brigade, the 1/45th, attacked and drove back the 103rd Line belonging to Remond's brigade of Darricau's division, suffering very few casualties in the process. Thus Picton's 3rd Division punched a huge hole through the centre of the main French position, and with the 4th Division and the Allied cavalry coming up fast, the French situation, already critical, suddenly became perilous.

Picton's thrust, coupled with Colville's advance, had caused Chasse's brigade to abandon its positions in and around the village of Margarita and it retired to the village of La Hermandad, a few hundred yards behind Margarita. Here it was joined by Neuenstein's German brigade, and together they made a stout defence as the Allies sought to turn the right of the new French line. Their assailants were Grant's brigade of the 7th Division, which had replaced Colville's, the latter having sustained some loss in its attempts to take Margarita. Grant's brigade was supported by Vandeleur's brigade of the Light Division.

ABOVE **A Connaught Ranger's view of the approach to Arinez with the village on the left and the heights of Puebla in the background. Once they had been driven out of the village the defenders formed up, briefly, on the low ridge which can be seen to the left of the village in this picture. Unfortunately, it lies to the south-east of the village whereas they should have ret-reated directly east. Thus, a gap began to open between Gazan and D'Erlon.**

The fight for La Hermandad was to be a far more severe affair, and Grant's men took heavy casualties from French artillery as they advanced across the open ground between Margarita and La Hermandad. Indeed, the attack stalled as Dalhousie, who had himself come forward, took cover with Grant's men in a ditch some 200 yards from the village. French shells were exploding all around Dalhousie and his staff as they debated what to do next, when suddenly Vandeleur's brigade of the Light Division – the 1/52nd and 2/95th – swept past them, gathering up the stalled battalions of the 7th Division as they went, and hit La Hermandad with such force that within about ten minutes the German defenders were driven out on to the higher ground behind.

The capture of La Hermandad compromised the right flank of the second French position, causing them to re-align once again. A new position was now taken up by the French, the right flank resting on the Zadorra at the village of Crispiana, running south to Zuazo, situated on a low ridge, and continuing on across the main road as far as the village

Wellington was never blessed with too many guns in the Peninsula, but at Vittoria he gathered together over 70 guns to pound the French line. Opposed to these were a similar number of French guns which led to a great artillery duel during the afternoon, the greatest of the Peninsular War. Wellington would never have as many guns in battle until Waterloo in 1815.

of Esquivel. The problem here was that while Vandeleur and Colville had been forcing the right flank of the French line, Hill's men, high upon the heights of Puebla, had been forcing the left. Furthermore, the bulk of Wellington's own command had crossed the Zadorra at Nanclares and Villodas and was beginning to push forward in the centre. The cavalry brigades of Robert Hill, Ponsonby, Victor Alten and Grant, as well as D'Urban's Portuguese, were all now on the right bank of the Zadorra, as was Cole's 4th Division. Colonel Alexander Dickson, commanding the artillery, had also moved forward and had begun bringing up all his guns in order to pound the centre of the French line.

The artillery duel between Dickson's 75 guns and the 76 French guns under General Tirlet was by far the greatest of the entire war. Wellington had never before enjoyed such a large number of pieces, and would not again until Waterloo, two years later. It was around 4.00pm when Wellington began to array his guns for what he must have known would be the decisive stroke to break Joseph's army.

The French position now extended for about two miles, from Crispiana on the right, held by Cassagne's division, along the low ridge to the village of Zuazo, held by Darmagnac's division, over the main road through Gomecha, held by Leval, and on to Esquivel, held by Villatte. However, the problem was that they had never really settled down into position, having been forced to fight and disengage under severe pressure from Allied infantry and artillery fire, since Dickson's guns were now forward. Furthermore, taking up a new position on ground which had not previously been surveyed was fraught with dangers.

Shortly after 4.00pm Wellington deployed his infantry for the final push against a weakening French line. The Allies drew up in a long line which began opposite Crispiana on the left and stretched as far as the ground in front of Esquivel on the right. The Allied order from left to

BELOW **Another view of the battle, this time with much more smoke, which was probably the case, particularly once Dickson's 75 guns opened fire en masse against the 76 French guns opposed to them. It was the greatest artillery duel of the war.**

ABOVE **The heights of Puebla, looking west from the hills to the south of Gomecha, Gazan's final position. The village in the distance is Zumelzu.**

right was Grant, Power, Brisbane, Stubbs, Byng and O'Callaghan. The latter two brigades had been fighting along the valley floor and lower slopes of the Puebla heights since the opening of the battle, and had suffered heavy casualties. Supporting this first line were the brigades of Vandeleur, Kempt, W. Anson, Skerrett and Ashworth, with the cavalry at the rear. It must have been a formidable sight: this massive array of troops making its way forward as enemy shells exploded around them and round shot ploughed huge lanes through them. The amount of iron poured into the Allied ranks brought the advance to a halt and then threw it back, but once Dickson's guns had been brought up to reply, the French guns slackened and the Allies resumed their advance. This time there was no stopping them: the vice had begun to tighten around the French. Not only were Cameron's men beginning to descend from the heights of Puebla to take Gazan in his left flank, but a gap had opened up along the main road, caused by Leval's withdrawal south-east instead of east from Arinez. This meant that instead of pre-

ABOVE **The battle of Vittoria. British infantry wait to attack whilst long lines of their comrades can be seen advancing in the background. Vittoria itself lies in the distance.**

ABOVE **A view looking west from the final French position on the slopes between Ali and Armentia with the heights of Puebla to the left. Wellington's infantry came on towards this position under heavy artillery fire from over 30 guns placed along these slopes.**

senting a continuous front there was a noticeable gap north of the main road between Gomecha and Zuazo. Into this gap moved Allied troops, outflanking Gazan to the south of the main road and D'Erlon, who was holding on at Zuazo. D'Erlon's left flank had been left unprotected by Leval's withdrawal, so there was little option but to begin pulling back.

Things were bad enough along the length of the line held by the Army of the South and the Army of the Centre, but then a rumour began to spread along the line that the great road to Bayonne had been cut at Durana. Not only was the main escape route back to France blocked, but there was also a very real possibility that the Allies would soon be attacking the French from the rear if they got across the Zadorra to the northeast of Vittoria.

The fight for Gamarra Mayor had reached a stalemate, with Graham's troops, the 5th Division, in possession of the village yet unable to cross the bridge over the Zadorra because French guns covered it. The same was true at Durana, where Longa's Spaniards found themselves unable to advance beyond the immediate area around the bridge because of stiff French resistance. In Graham's sector the village of Abechuco had been cleared of French defenders without any serious loss, but Graham decided not to try the bridges over the Zadorra either at Yurre, which lay further to the west, or between Abechuco and Arriaga. This meant that the bulk of his British and Portuguese troops, nearly 8,000 in all, were left kicking their heels in frustration all day. Indeed, the total loss in casualties at Vittoria in the 1st Division numbered just 54, ample indication of their inactivity during the day. We know that Graham had been ordered by Wellington not to get too involved in the fighting to the north of Vittoria lest it draw down upon him large French reserves and in so doing compromise his main task of cutting the road to France. Yet

MORILLO'S MEN ON THE HEIGHTS OF PUEBLA
Along with Cadogan's brigade, Morillo's Spanish division began the battle of Vittoria by clearing the heights of Puebla of French defenders and thus made a major contribution to Wellington's victory. The lofty heights were cleared gradually

from west to east until the Allied troops poured down from them just to the south of Vittoria itself at the point when Gazan's Army of the South was making good its retreat to the east. Morillo himself was badly wounded early in the fight.

with so few French troops opposing – of which he was probably unaware – he could have made matters far worse for both Gazan and D'Erlon had he brushed aside the French defenders at Yurre and Arriaga and pushed on into the rear of the main French position.

At Durana, meanwhile, the fight for the village was coming to the boil. It was at around 5.00pm when Longa's men finally drove the defenders from the bridge and stormed into the village. After some confused fighting at close quarters in the small streets, it finally fell to the Allies. However, Longa could not push on into the French rear because the exits from the village were covered by Casapalicios's guns. He had, nevertheless, accomplished his main task of cutting the great road to France.

At Gamarra Mayor Robinson's brigade had made repeated efforts to cross the bridge but with little success; instead there was an ever-growing number of bodies in the village's narrow streets. Eventually Oswald was forced to pull out Robinson's battle-weary men and send in the 3/1st and Spry's Portuguese. These too failed to get beyond the bridge but were simply cut down whenever they set foot on the southern bank of the river. There was no cover whatsoever on the French-held side of the bank and even with Oswald's men in possession of the bridge Reille's men could feel fairly satisfied with the state of affairs in front of them and confident that as long as their guns continued sweeping the exits from the bridge, there was no need to fear danger. (There were no fords nearby either.) Reille would continue to hold back the Allies in this sector until the collapse of the French army behind him.

Along the high road, meanwhile, things were turning from bad to worse for Joseph. The withdrawal from Arinez to the south-east by Leval's troops had opened up a gap into which Allied skirmishers began to pour, leading the way for the main Allied troops. Gazan, commanding the Army of the South, saw what was coming and, without thought for D'Erlon and the Army of the Centre still fighting along the centre of the valley floor, decided – without orders – to retreat to the east. He could see the Allies skirting round his right flank, and with Cameron's men beginning to appear on his left, he gave the order to fall back from the position which he was holding along the Gomecha–Esquivel line. One can understand his reasoning: both his flanks had been turned, though this was partly his own fault. After Leval had been thrown out of Arinez, he should have retreated directly east along the high road, aligning himself with D'Erlon's left flank which was anchored around Zuazo. As his commanding officer, Gazan should have ordered Leval to plug the gap instead of allowing him to drift off to the south of the high road. After all, Gazan would have had a perfect viewpoint in his position on the heights above Gomecha, and must surely have seen the consequences which would arise from the mistake. It was not to be, however, and not wishing to be cut off, Gazan gave the order to retreat.

This unauthorised withdrawal seriously compromised D'Erlon, whose left flank was thus hanging while the 2nd and 4th divisions of Wellington's army bore down on the gap along the high road. In truth, the game had probably been up for the French from the moment Picton turned Leval out of Arinez to pierce the French left centre, and with the Allies driving along the top of the heights of Puebla, there was little prospect of Gazan maintaining his position with his left being turned. However, he demonstrated a complete lack of loyalty both to D'Erlon and to Joseph: instead of shoring up the gap in the line and moving to his right to assist the Army of the Centre, he simply left them to it and made off to the east without even being hard pressed by the Allies. While Gazan was not the villain of the whole piece, he deserved a large share of the blame for the disaster which was unfolding.

Meanwhile, D'Erlon was fighting desperately to hold back the tide of Allied troops driving east along the valley floor. With Gazan having departed on his left, there was little prospect of him succeeding. His men were swept from both Crispiana and Zuazo, forcing him to occupy a line from Ali to Armentia – his final position during the battle. To his credit, D'Erlon continued fighting to hold back the 3rd Division, even though the 2nd and 4th divisions were threatening his left. He had with him over 30 guns, which played havoc among the ranks of the 3rd Division. However, D'Erlon was undone, once again, by a flanking move which took Grant, Colville and Vandeleur around his right flank, past the village of Ali. D'Erlon and the Army of the Centre were now outflanked on both sides. Furthermore, the advance of the three British brigades along the Zadorra would shortly bring them into contact with Graham's troops, still engaged with Reille and the Army of Portugal, to the north of Vittoria. D'Erlon was no fool, and he could see that the situation was hopeless, so it was no surprise when, at around 5.30pm, an orderly rode up bearing a message from Joseph himself, ordering a general retreat.

BELOW **British infantry going into action at Vittoria.**

VITTORIA: PHASE III 1700-1900

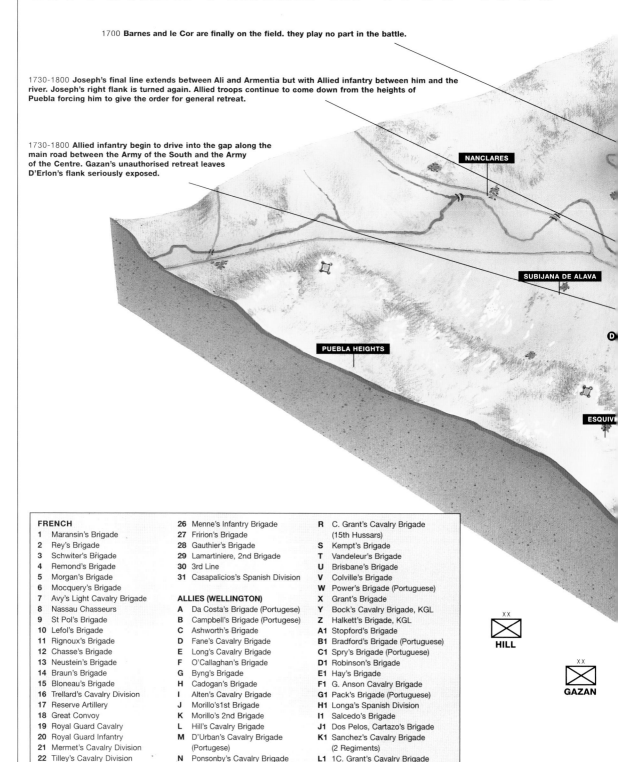

1700 **Barnes and le Cor are finally on the field. they play no part in the battle.**

1730-1800 **Joseph's final line extends between Ali and Armentia but with Allied infantry between him and the river. Joseph's right flank is turned again. Allied troops continue to come down from the heights of Puebla forcing him to give the order for general retreat.**

1730-1800 **Allied infantry begin to drive into the gap along the main road between the Army of the South and the Army of the Centre. Gazan's unauthorised retreat leaves D'Erlon's flank seriously exposed.**

NANCLARES

SUBIJANA DE ALAVA

PUEBLA HEIGHTS

D

ESQUIV

X X
HILL

X X
GAZAN

FRENCH
1. Maransin's Brigade
2. Rey's Brigade
3. Schwiter's Brigade
4. Remond's Brigade
5. Morgan's Brigade
6. Mocquery's Brigade
7. Avy's Light Cavalry Brigade
8. Nassau Chasseurs
9. St Pol's Brigade
10. Lefol's Brigade
11. Rignoux's Brigade
12. Chasse's Brigade
13. Neustein's Brigade
14. Braun's Brigade
15. Bloneau's Brigade
16. Trellard's Cavalry Division
17. Reserve Artillery
18. Great Convoy
19. Royal Guard Cavalry
20. Royal Guard Infantry
21. Mermet's Cavalry Division
22. Tilley's Cavalry Division
23. Curto's, 2nd Brigade Light Cavalry
24. Digeon's Cavalry Division
25. Curto's 1t cavalry Brigade

26. Menne's Infantry Brigade
27. Fririon's Brigade
28. Gauthier's Brigade
29. Lamartiniere, 2nd Brigade
30. 3rd Line
31. Casapalicios's Spanish Division

ALLIES (WELLINGTON)
A. Da Costa's Brigade (Portugese)
B. Campbell's Brigade (Portugese)
C. Ashworth's Brigade
D. Fane's Cavalry Brigade
E. Long's Cavalry Brigade
F. O'Callaghan's Brigade
G. Byng's Brigade
H. Cadogan's Brigade
I. Alten's Cavalry Brigade
J. Morillo's1st Brigade
K. Morillo's 2nd Brigade
L. Hill's Cavalry Brigade
M. D'Urban's Cavalry Brigade (Portugese)
N. Ponsonby's Cavalry Brigade
O. Stubb's Brigade (Portugese)
P. Skerrett's Brigade
Q. W. Anson's Brigade

R. C. Grant's Cavalry Brigade (15th Hussars)
S. Kempt's Brigade
T. Vandeleur's Brigade
U. Brisbane's Brigade
V. Colville's Brigade
W. Power's Brigade (Portuguese)
X. Grant's Brigade
Y. Bock's Cavalry Brigade, KGL
Z. Halkett's Brigade, KGL
A1. Stopford's Brigade
B1. Bradford's Brigade (Portuguese)
C1. Spry's Brigade (Portuguese)
D1. Robinson's Brigade
E1. Hay's Brigade
F1. G. Anson Cavalry Brigade
G1. Pack's Brigade (Portuguese)
H1. Longa's Spanish Division
I1. Salcedo's Brigade
J1. Dos Pelos, Cartazo's Brigade
K1. Sanchez's Cavalry Brigade (2 Regiments)
L1. 1C. Grant's Cavalry Brigade (10th & 11th Hussars)
M1. Lecor Brigade
N1. Barne's Brigade

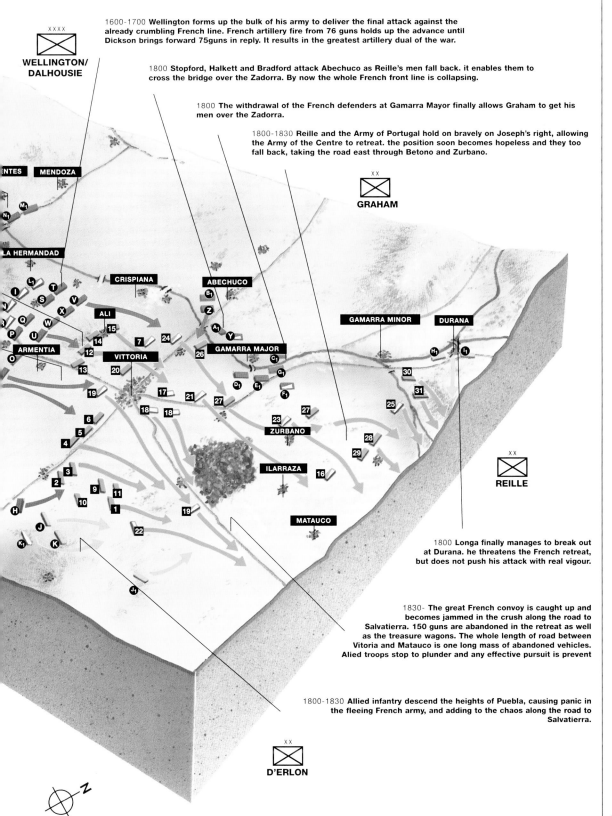

1600-1700 Wellington forms up the bulk of his army to deliver the final attack against the already crumbling French line. French artillery fire from 76 guns holds up the advance until Dickson brings forward 75guns in reply. It results in the greatest artillery dual of the war.

1800 Stopford, Halkett and Bradford attack Abechuco as Reille's men fall back. it enables them to cross the bridge over the Zadorra. By now the whole French front line is collapsing.

1800 The withdrawal of the French defenders at Gamarra Mayor finally allows Graham to get his men over the Zadorra.

1800-1830 Reille and the Army of Portugal hold on bravely on Joseph's right, allowing the Army of the Centre to retreat. the position soon becomes hopeless and they too fall back, taking the road east through Betono and Zurbano.

WELLINGTON/
DALHOUSIE
XXXX

GRAHAM
X X

NTES
MENDOZA
LA HERMANDAD
CRISPIANA
ABECHUCO
GAMARRA MINOR
DURANA
ALI
GAMARRA MAJOR
ARMENTIA
VITTORIA
ZURBANO
ILARRAZA
MATAUCO
REILLE
X X

1800 Longa finally manages to break out at Durana. he threatens the French retreat, but does not push his attack with real vigour.

1830- The great French convoy is caught up and becomes jammed in the crush along the road to Salvatierra. 150 guns are abandoned in the retreat as well as the treasure wagons. The whole length of road between Vitoria and Matauco is one long mass of abandoned vehicles. Alied troops stop to plunder and any effective pursuit is prevent

1800-1830 Allied infantry descend the heights of Puebla, causing panic in the fleeing French army, and adding to the chaos along the road to Salvatierra.

D'ERLON
X X

THE FRENCH RETREAT

The process of disengaging from an enemy advancing in overwhelming strength is a dangerous business at the best of times. At Vittoria it was particularly tricky for the French because the main – and logical – escape route back to France had been cut by Longa's men earlier in the afternoon. The only way out lay along the Salvatierra road which led to Pamplona, and this was by no means in good condition. Joseph ordered D'Erlon and the Army of the Centre to retreat by the tracks that ran to the north of Vittoria in order to avoid coming into collision with Gazan's retreating Army of the South, which had retired to the south of Vittoria. This left Reille and the Army of Portugal with the unenviable task of holding back Graham's men until the last of D'Erlon's troops had passed to their rear. He was then to fall back himself, passing to the east of Vittoria. With D'Erlon's right flank turned, however, the more immediate threat to Reille was to his left rear, as British troops began to push east from beyond the village of Ali. There was little point in remaining, so in spite of orders to stay where he was until the Army of the Centre had passed, Reille ordered an immediate withdrawal from the positions along the Zadorra. This was not easy because his men were engaged along a front stretching from Arriaga on his left to Durana on his right. Moreover, Oswald and the 5th Division were still pressing at Gamarra Mayor, while Longa's Spaniards were waiting to explode onto the main battlefield, having been penned in at Durana. In spite of these difficulties, Reille extricated his troops with great skill, making good use of Digeon's cavalry to hold back the British light dragoons and hussars, who now began to make their presence felt. It was certainly a close call at Arriaga, on Reille's left, where Menne's infantry brigade escaped by the skin of their teeth from the clutches of the 15th Hussars, who swept up from the south and tried to cut them off. This was accomplished at great cost, however, for not only were they forced to leave all their guns behind in and around Arriaga, but they also lost General Sarrut, a Peninsular veteran and Menne's divisional commander. Sarrut was mortally wounded as his men began to retreat.

Just under a mile to the north-east of Vittoria lay the small village of Betono, in front of which Reille had drawn up Fririon's brigade in reserve. This now served as a rallying point for both Menne and Digeon, as they hurried east, to the north of Vittoria. While D'Erlon's men made their way to the south of the village, the brigades of Menne and Fririon, supported by the cavalry brigades of Digeon, Boyer and Curto, prepared to make their last stand to allow Lamartiniere to withdraw safely from Gamarra Mayor. This hazardous undertaking went quite smoothly, and the French troops pulled back from the bridge, followed shortly afterwards by men of Oswald's 5th Division, came spilling across the Zadorra in hot pursuit. At Durana, meanwhile, the Franco-Spanish troops under Casapalicios simply made off across the hilltops to the north-east of Vittoria, with Longa's men following them.

ABOVE **The church in the village of Ali, Joseph's final position from where he gave the final order for a general retreat.**

RIGHT **A view from the final French position between Ali and Armentia, looking towards the hills to the south of Gomecha. Armentia, in fact, can be seen on the left. It was here that the junction of the Armies of the South and Centre should have been but, owing to the misdirected withdrawal of Leval, a gap opened instead, through which the Allies poured, precipitating the total collapse of Joseph's forces.**

ABOVE **A French square attempts to stem the Allied advance whilst resistance begins to collapse around it.**

Joseph's army now faced the difficult task of extricating itself from the valley floor which was, in effect, partially blocked by the town of Vittoria itself. The French also had a mass of impedimenta with them – the huge treasure convoy, wagons, the baggage train, the artillery park and the guns. It was the chaos caused by this massive obstruction, combined with the total rout of Joseph's army, that led to the incredible scenes of disorder and unbridled anarchy.

Wellington's army came on like a steamroller, crushing any resistance that was offered as the remnants of Joseph's armies fled east. To the north of Vittoria D'Erlon's troops were retreating in total disarray across fields and along bad tracks, with the 3rd Division in hot pursuit.

One has to feel for Reille, bravely standing at Betono, waiting for Lamartiniere to come in from Gamarra Mayor. Reille had held back Graham's corps along the Zadorra long enough for D'Erlon to make good his escape. Now, however, it was his own turn, for no sooner had Lamartiniere arrived than Reille pulled back from Betono towards the small village of Zurbano, about two miles east of Vittoria. He was pursued by Graham's entire corps, which had crossed the Zadorra as soon as Reille

69

abandoned the bridges. The pursuit was led by one squadron each of the 12th and 16th light dragoons, who came upon Reille's rearguard just as it reached Zurbano, having cleared a wood to its west. Initially the British light dragoons were repulsed by a combination of dragoons and hussars, but after re-forming they charged again: this time they were successful. After driving off the French cavalry, the light dragoons came across the 36th Line, part of Fririon's brigade, drawn up in square just outside the village. As was often the case in such a situation, it was the infantry who won the encounter, and the British cavalry were

driven off by steady musketry. This allowed Reille to get most of his infantry safely across the fields and paths to the north of the road to Salvatierra. In so doing he avoided the congestion and disorder along a great length of the road east of Vittoria. Reille also managed to get two of Lamartiniere's six guns – incredibly the only two guns the French managed to get away from the battlefield out of a total of 153. Here the pursuit slackened, the 5th Division having exhausted itself during the day and in the relatively short pursuit afterwards. Indeed, the 5th Division camped that night just outside Zurbano, and the 1st Division camped nearer the Zadorra. Reille was never threatened again by the Allies, although some of Longa's men coming over the hills east of Durana opened fire from some distance on his fleeing columns.

Elsewhere things were not going so well for the French. To the south of Vittoria Gazan's Army of the South was streaming away across land crossed by bad tracks which for the most part ran north–south instead of

BELOW **Wellington (centre) with some of his men during the closing stages of the battle. French troops fight to bring away one of their 'eagles' as British troops close in on them. French chests (left) have already been opened and plundered.**

ABOVE The road to Salvatierra, looking back towards Vittoria, from the village of Ilarraza. It was here in these fields that much of the great French convoy was abandoned to the pursuing Allies, thus choking the escape route to Pamplona. These fields were the scenes of the great plundering of the treasure wagons after the battle.

east–west. Thus the fugitives were forced to take to the countryside in their bid for freedom. There was little time for an organised flight: it was simply a case of every man for himself. Weapons and equipment were cast off and baggage wagons abandoned, while guns and ammunition wagons were left standing in fields. The few guns which the French did attempt to move quickly became stuck in the boggy ground and had to be left to the Allied troops. In fact, Gazan gave orders for the abandonment of all of his artillery. Meanwhile, Cameron and Morillo's troops, having poured down from the eastern end of the heights of Puebla, spread even greater panic in the French ranks as they began to press after the rear of the fugitives, and when the first pistols were heard from Wellington's cavalry – Grant's hussars took a short cut through the suburbs of Vittoria – all hell was let loose.

The French problem stemmed from the size of their convoy. It was vast, and it is worth taking a look at just what it included. The great convoy had begun to accumulate in March 1813 when, in compliance with Napoleon's orders, Joseph left Madrid and moved his headquarters to Valladolid. Rightly judging the move to be the last time he would see Madrid, he decided to take with him paintings, libraries, jewels of all size and description, money, collections of furniture and antiques and the accumulated plunder of five years of French occupation of Spain. Besides this load there was Joseph's entourage, the government and its ministers, secretaries, servants, hangers-on, civilians and their wives and families and the families of the soldiers themselves. This extraordinary convoy had increased as it moved further north, attracting more and more French officials and lackeys. By the time it reached Vittoria it is estimated to have consisted of some 3,000 carriages and to have stretched about 12 miles. Added to this was the array of army equipment, the reserve artillery, ammunition wagons, supplies, ambulances, field forges and other sundry equipment. Then there were the carriages which had arrived from France on 19 June containing no less than five and a half million gold francs for the royal treasury. What a prize this was to become for the infamously voracious soldiers of Wellington's army. The situation could have been worse for the French after Vittoria had part of the convoy not been sent off along the great road to France on 19 June, under the command of General Rey, who was shortly after to assume command of the garrison of San Sebastian. As we have seen, Maucune had already left, on the morning of the battle, with another part of the convoy. However, this still left around 2,000 vehicles clogging up the exits from Vittoria to the east of the town as well as the great host of non-military personnel, all of whom had followed the progress of the battle with growing anxiety. As the first Allied shells began to explode around Vittoria, their anxiety quickly turned into hysteria and panic, which heightened as the first troops of Gazan's Army of the South began to stream past them from the battlefield. All of this only served to increase the blockage along the narrow Salvatierra road, which was the only direction of salvation for Joseph's beaten forces.

Joseph himself had fled the battlefield around 6.00pm and along with Jourdan tried to instil some semblance of order into the chaos raging around him. He sent aides off into the mayhem, but without any success. Joseph's aides were simply swept along by the tide of panic. Realising that there was nothing further he could do, Joseph jumped into his carriage and tried to make good his escape. Soon afterwards, however, he found himself and his entourage firmly stuck in the midst of the heaving, panic-stricken throng of battle-field refugees. Soon the cry went up that British hussars were upon them. These were Grant's cavalry, the 10th, 15th and 18th hussars, who came sweeping around to the north of Vittoria (some accounts say they went through the town) and charged east straight into the rear of the confusion. In spite of the chaos, some French units tried to resist Grant's cavalry, in particular some of Joseph's Royal Guard as well as the 5th Chasseurs and the 4th and 26th dragoons. They could not stop the British hussars, however. Captain Windham of the 10th Hussars reached Joseph's carriage at the precise moment that the king was leaping out of the other door. Joseph avoided capture by a whisker, leaving behind him his sword, seals, some clothing, jewels and his chamber pot! Jourdan too lost several personal possessions, including his Marshal's baton. This was taken by a corporal of the 18th Hussars and later sent by Wellington to the Prince Regent.

Wellington's cavalry at Vittoria had hardly been engaged all day, but now, with the routed French army in full flight, they were needed to carry out the pursuit. It was a perfect opportunity for them to demonstrate what they could do, for never before on the field of battle in the Peninsula had

ABOVE **British cavalry capture Joseph's carriage during the closing stages of the battle of Vittoria. Captain Wyndham, of the 10th Hussars, actually took hold of one of the doors of Joseph's carriage at the moment when the king himself was in the act of jumping out the other side.**

this most delicate arm been in such great strength. Yet the opportunity was lost because of the old malaise of the British soldier – the desire for plunder. This was not confined to the mounted arm of the army, for the infantry also stopped to fill their pockets. Thus the French were allowed to get away in far greater strength than they might have.

THE PURSUIT STALLS

The aftermath of the battle of Vittoria is well known. Wellington's men were met by an astonishing scene as they pursued the French army: fields covered in the abandoned wreckage of Joseph's great convoy of treasure – silks, books, paintings and jewels, all mixed with the flotsam and jetsam of war. The looting of the convoy began, however, with the fleeing French soldiers, who plundered their own wagons. Wellington's men simply came upon them and joined in. As at Ciudad Rodrigo and Badajoz, it was not unusual for both friend and foe to be seen tearing open wooden chests and sharing out their contents.

It is said that never before had such a vast haul of treasure been taken by a victorious army on the field of battle, and certainly there is some justification in this. By far the most important wagons – as far as Wellington was concerned – were those which had arrived from France on 19 June carrying the millions of francs of French subsidy. Wellington had hoped that this would fill his own military chest and bring his men's arrears of pay into line, but he was to be sadly disappointed, for just 250,000 francs were recovered, the rest was spirited away by the soldiers. Joseph's treasurer, Thiebault, was shot dead in the act of defending a box containing 100,000 francs. It was not only cash and treasures that were taken either: Gazan's wife, the Countess Gazan, was captured in her carriage, but she was treated well and was sent to rejoin her husband.

There is little doubt that had it not been for the incredible amount of treasure discarded, Wellington's army would have been able to inflict a far greater loss on the French. But it was not to be. An extremely angry Wellington summed up the position perfectly when he wrote: 'The night of the battle, instead of being passed in getting rest and food to prepare them for the pursuit of the following day, was passed by the soldiers in looking for plunder. The consequence was that they were incapable of marching in pursuit of the enemy, and were totally knocked up.' The episode also led to another, even more famous, outburst, in which Wellington called some of his men 'the scum of the earth'.

The gloss was certainly taken off Wellington's victory at Vittoria by the lack of an effective pursuit, but it was a crushing victory nevertheless. The Allies suffered just over 5,000 casualties – 3,672 were British, including 509 killed, 921 were Portuguese and 522 Spaniards. The French lost just over 8,000 men – 42 officers and 716 men killed, 226 officers and 4,210 men wounded, and 23 officers and 2,825 men taken prisoner. Surprisingly, no French 'eagles' were taken at Vittoria, but the treasure taken afterwards more than compensated for the lack of imperial trinkets.

ABOVE **The auction after the battle of Vittoria, after a drawing by Wollen. Such auctions were typical after battles, when dead soldiers' belongings were auctioned off, often to pay for outstanding expenses. The aftermath of Vittoria, however, took such auctions to new heights with an unparalleled amount of plunder offered for sale.**

THE PURSUIT TO FRANCE

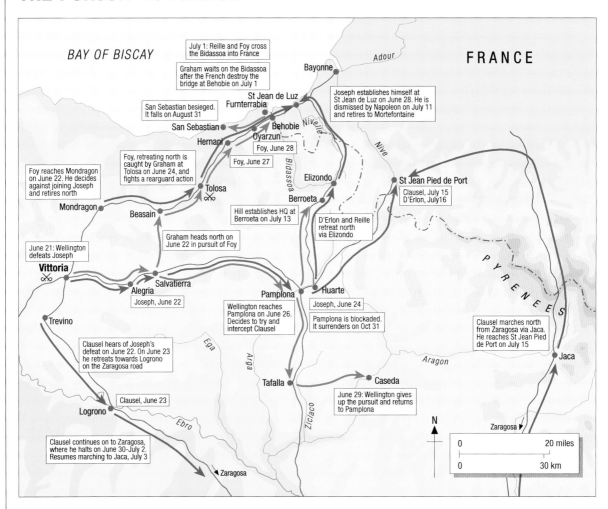

BAY OF BISCAY

FRANCE

Adour

July 1: Reille and Foy cross the Bidassoa into France

Graham waits on the Bidassoa after the French destroy the bridge at Behobie on July 1

Joseph establishes himself at St Jean de Luz on June 28. He is dismissed by Napoleon on July 11 and retires to Mortefontaine

San Sebastian besieged. It falls on August 31

St Jean de Luz
Furnterrabia
Behobie
Nivelle
Nive

San Sebastian
Hernani
Oyarzun
Foy, June 28

Foy, retreating north is caught by Graham at Tolosa on June 24, and fights a rearguard action

Foy, June 27

Elizondo

St Jean Pied de Port

Clausel, July 15
D'Erlon, July16

Foy reaches Mondragon on June 22. He decides against joining Joseph and retires north

Tolosa

Berroeta

Mondragon
Beasain

Hill establishes HQ at Berroeta on July 13

D'Erlon and Reille retreat north via Elizondo

June 21: Wellington defeats Joseph

Graham heads north on June 22 in pursuit of Foy

P Y R E N E E S

Vittoria

Salvatierra
Alegria
Joseph, June 22

Pamplona
Huarte
Joseph, June 24

Clausel marches north from Zaragosa via Jaca. He reaches St Jean Pied de Port on July 15

Trevino

Wellington reaches Pamplona on June 26. Decides to try and intercept Clausel

Pamplona is blockaded. It surrenders on Oct 31

Jaca

Clausel hears of Joseph's defeat on June 22. On June 23 he retreats towards Logrono on the Zaragosa road

Ega
Arga
Aragon

Caseda

Tafalla

June 29: Wellington gives up the pursuit and returns to Pamplona

Clausel, June 23

Ziciaco

N

Zaragosa ▶

Logrono

Ebro

Clausel continues on to Zaragosa, where he halts on June 30-July 2. Resumes marching to Jaca, July 3

Zaragosa

0	20 miles
0	30 km

AFTERMATH

The remnants of the French army at Vittoria hurried away to the east after the battle, an escape made easier by the inability of Wellington's men to perform an effective pursuit. Clausel, meanwhile, remained in complete ignorance of the disaster and, even as Wellington's men were busy plundering the abandoned French wagons, was hurrying north, via Logrono, to link up with Joseph. It came as quite a shock, therefore, when on 23 June his cavalry patrols returned with news of the defeat and reported that the area was crawling with British troops. These were men from the 6th Division, which had taken no part in the fighting but had followed up as the main army headed east. Clausel immediately returned the way he had come, taking the road to Zaragosa where he hoped to join Suchet. Wellington tried to intercept him with the 6th Division, but Clausel, finding that Suchet had already left Zaragosa, managed to elude the British and slipped back into France via the Pyrenees.

Foy too had a narrow escape. Like Clausel, he had taken no part in the battle. He was marching south towards Vittoria when he received news of Joseph's defeat. He too did an about-turn and headed for France, taking the Tolosa road, but he was caught by Graham, who had gone in pursuit of him. There followed a stiff fight between Graham's force and Foy's rearguard, but the experienced French general managed to extricate himself and continued north, dropping off reinforcements for the garrison at San Sebastian before crossing the Bidassoa and entering France.

After narrowly avoiding capture at Vittoria, Joseph had gone east to Pamplona. He arrived on 24 June, and from here he travelled north, over the Pyrenees, and returned to France. After facing his brother's wrath he returned to his estate at Mortefontaine but was later placed in command of the Paris National Guard. Jourdan went to France with Joseph and took most of the blame for the French defeat at Vittoria. He never saw action again, and retired from service. He died 20 years after his greatest defeat.

With both Joseph and Jourdan recalled to France, command of the French army, which now faced the threat of an Allied invasion, was given to Marshal Soult, who had been recalled to France the previous year in readiness for the German campaign. Soult, who had been in the Peninsula from 1808, failed to do to Wellington what he had done to Sir John Moore in 1809, namely to drive him into the

BELOW **A view of the bridge at Durana. Longa's men reached the bridge early in the afternoon but could not cross it for some time. When they finally took the bridge and Durana itself, they still found it impossible to debouch from it owing to heavy French artillery fire which kept them penned in.**

ABOVE **The flight of King Joseph from Vittoria. After a painting by Granville Baker. A somewhat stylised version of Joseph's flight, as his carriage trundles off the battlefield surrounded by his bodyguard and pursued by British infantry. In fact, Joseph's carriage was taken in the flat fields to the east of Vittoria**

sea. Circumstances had changed dramatically since the winter of 1808/9, but Soult still managed to cause Wellington more than one problem in the remaining months of the war.

If Wellington's victory at Vittoria effectively ended French aspirations in Spain, it had even greater repercussions elsewhere in Europe. Indeed, it brought an end to the Armistice of Pleishwitz, which had been signed on 4 June 1813 between Napoleon and his Austrian, Prussian and Russian enemies, following the battles of Lutzen and Bautzen and the French capture of Dresden. All combatant nations, who suffered equally following the battles, had sought the armistice, but, largely through the efforts of Castlereagh, both Russia and Prussia, along with Sweden, were persuaded to press for a resumption of hostilities. Only Austria was uncommitted. However, upon learning of the French disaster at Vittoria, the British government went to great lengths to ensure that news of it reached the Austrians. (Napoleon having done his best to suppress it.) Upon hearing of Wellington's victory, the Austrians decided to take up arms once again, and on 12 August 1813 they declared war on France. Thus Vittoria had much more far-reaching consequences than Wellington could have imagined.

The morale of the French army was severely shattered by its defeat at Vittoria, and one of Soult's major tasks was to restore some semblance of order and belief to its ranks. His counter-offensive of July 1813 in the Pyrenees demonstrated that the French soldier possessed the ability to recover quickly. Indeed, the offensive almost succeeded in relieving the beleaguered city of Pamplona, and there was much hard fighting to do before Wellington ended the war successfully for the Allies.

San Sebastian fell to the Allies on 31 August, although the garrison and its commander, Rey, remained within the castle above the town until 7 September. In October Pamplona fell, and with it the last French-held fortress was reclaimed by the Allies. On 7 October Wellington launched his men across the Bidassoa. In so doing he finally set foot on the 'sacred soil' of France after years of slog across the Peninsula. Possibly his greatest victory was achieved on 10 November at the battle of the Nivelle. Indeed, years afterwards Wellington claimed that battle as his finest accomplishment. It was certainly a masterpiece, as he brought his attacking columns to bear on the French positions in overwhelming strength, rolling back, in Napier's words, 'Soult's iron barrier as if it were a screen of reeds'. By the end of the year Wellington's forces were blockading Bayonne, the great French military base in south-west France. February 1814 saw his men cross the river Adour, and while an Allied force stayed behind around Bayonne, Wellington's field army headed east into the French interior in pursuit of Soult. They caught up

BELOW **Another caricature by Cruikshank. In this cartoon, a French general, trying to make off with a large rib of beef, pleads with John Bull to be allowed just a little piece. 'No, no, I'll be damned if you take the roast beef with you,' comes the reply from a bayonet-wielding British soldier.**

ABOVE **One of the many contemporary prints depicting Wellington's victories in the Peninsula. The artist has managed to cram in as many of the separate episodes as he could, although nothing is really in order. Wellington sits on his horse, left, while Hill crosses a bridge on the right. Jourdan can be seen, top right, while British cavalry take possession of abandoned French guns and ammunition wagons.**

with him at Orthes, on 27 February 1814, and among the rolling fields Wellington won his last full-pitched battle of the war. There were smaller (though nonetheless sharp) actions at Aire and Tarbes before the final battle at Toulouse on 10 April 1814. Unknown to both sides, however, Napoleon had abdicated some days earlier. The final action of the Peninsular War came on 14 April 1814: a futile sortie by the governor of Bayonne, Thouvenot, formerly the governor of Vittoria, who attacked the blockading Allied force to the north of the town, causing heavy casualties for the Allies and his own attacking force.

The moment which ensured that the French would never achieve victory in the Peninsula came at Vittoria on 21 June 1813. Wellington's victory in Spain was decisive, but it would take a much more famous battle two years later – almost to the day – to bring about the final end to the Napoleonic dream.

THE PLUNDERING DURING THE AFTERMATH OF THE BATTLE

**The plundering of the great French convoy after the battle
of Vittoria ended all hopes Wellington must have harboured of an effective
pursuit by his army. However, although his anger is understandable it is
not surprising that his men stopped to plunder the convoy given the
incredible riches it contained. Fortunes were made by private soldiers and
officers alike from the spoils of victory while a furious Wellington had to
make do with a paltry 275,000 francs for his military chest out of a total of
5,500,000 with which he had hoped to bolster his flagging finances.**

THE BATTLEFIELD TODAY

The Vittoria campaign can be followed fairly satisfactorily from start to finish taking in both the movements of the Allied columns and the skirmishes along the way. Anybody wishing to 'begin at the beginning' is advised to start at Ciudad Rodrigo and follow the road east to Salamanca. There we are following Wellington and Hill with the right wing of the army. From Salamanca, head north to Toro and see the broken bridge, now repaired but still looking the worse for wear, before crossing to the north bank of the Douro. From Toro, head west, past Zamora, and travel out to Almendra, where Graham's wing of the army crossed the Esla. Today the crossing point bears no relation to that of 1813, since a dam has turned the river into something of a large lake. Return to Zamora and continue on to Morales. Take one of the sandy (but good) tracks east out of the town and follow it as far as the Bayas river, a small stream over which the old road to Pedrosa del Rey passes. By doing this you are following the course of the cavalry fight on 2 June. The ground has not changed, and it is most satisfactory to follow the fight as far as the heights on the right bank of the river, where the British hussars were brought up by enemy cavalry, infantry and artillery. Continuing north, follow the advance to Vittoria, travelling to the Puente Arenas, by which Hill crossed the Ebro. The more spectacular scenery is encountered by following Graham's column, particularly at San Martin de Lines. To get to this bridge you have to drive along the bottom of a gorge, above which tower castle-like rock formations which

BELOW **A view of the small village of La Hermandad, the scene of heavy fighting during the battle. It was finally taken by Vandeleur's brigade of the Light Division. Today, the village finds itself situated on the edge of an industrial estate.**

are mentioned in more than a few eye-witness accounts. The final approaches to Vittoria take you to San Milan and Osma. The former is particularly satisfying as the site of the action on 18 June has not changed much at all; neither has the position at Osma.

The battlefield of Vittoria itself is not one of the best-preserved battlefields in the Peninsula. Indeed, large areas of it have given way to

industrial estates or sports complexes. Fortunately, these areas are mainly confined to the central area of the battlefield in a sort of rectangle, with its boundaries roughly being Gomecha and La Hermandad in the west and the urban sprawl of Vittoria in the east, Vittoria having spread greatly since 1813. Much of the area within this boundary has been built over, although there are still areas which remain relatively untouched – Zuazo, for example, and the low range of hills on either side of it. Fortunately, most of the areas which saw hard fighting have escaped the developers.

There are two obvious places from which to begin any tour of the battlefield, one fairly easy to get to and the other much harder. The first is the knoll of Arinez, Joseph's initial command post. A track takes you to the top of this peculiar feature, which is split into two 'peaks'. Standing upon the western 'peak' of the knoll, one is afforded a great view of the area over which Wellington and Hill approached. Looking west, the villages of Nanclares and Villodas are easily visible, as is the entrance to the valley of the Zadorra, beneath the heights of Puebla. The heights themselves are visible from most places on the battlefield. A trip to the top of the knoll is vital in order to orientate oneself. Rotating through 360 degrees from the top of the eastern peak, one gets a view of the entire battlefield, save for the distant villages of Gamarra Mayor and Durana. In summer the heat haze often reduces visibility to such an extent that it is not possible to see even Vittoria, but in late autumn or winter it is often possible to see as far as the area around Gamarra Mayor and on to the hills beyond.

The other place to begin a tour of the battlefield is from the summit of the heights of Puebla. This is far more difficult to do, however, particularly by car, unless you ignore official signposts and warnings and take the very rough tracks that run to the huge television aerials from the southern side of the heights. Unless you have a four-wheel-drive vehicle or an armoured personnel carrier, I would advise against taking a vehicle to the top. There are tracks that run from

Subjiana de Alava, Zumelzu and Esquivel that take you to the summit, but this is only possible on foot. It is a fairly stiff walk to the top, but from there it is pos-sible to get a magnificent bird's-eye-view of the battlefield. It is necessary to walk quite a length of the heights in order to see the entire length of the battlefield, because some of the peaks prevent a complete overview from a single point. Of course, by climbing to the top of the heights it is possible to appreciate the task carried out by both Cadogan's and Morillo's men, who fought their way across this steep, rocky hillside. The fault where the 71st came unstuck is also easy to locate, with its very steep sides which must have been a great effort to climb, let alone fight on. A walk along the heights also highlights just how perilous the French position was once the Allies began driving along, outflanking each successive position. (It is little wonder that Jourdan thought that the attack along the heights represented the main Allied effort.)

An aerial view of the centre of the battlefield of Vittoria, looking to the north, taken some years ago during the construction of the industrial estates. The two villages on the left, separated by the new motorway, are Margarita and La Hermandad. The village, just visible on the left-hand edge of the picture, is Mendoza. Both Picton and Dalhousie debouched from the hills in the background. An airfield has been built on the battlefield, visible on the right, although there was no fighting on the ground on which it was built. When Wellington launched his final infantry attack, supported by Dickson's guns, it stretched from the Zadorra, marked by the tree-line two-thirds of the way up this picture, right down to the high road, which lies out of shot, far to the south of this area. The Allied line swept across this ground from left to right and was one of the great sights of the war.

The bridges over the Zadorra at Nanclares, Villodas and Tres Puentes are still there, although the bridge crossed by Wellington and the 4th Division has been modernised. The bridges at Villodas and Tres Puentes are those of 1813, but the bridge crossed by Picton's 3rd Division has been modernised. The area fought over by the 3rd Division and the Light Division is perhaps the most evocative. Indeed, it is pos-sible to walk across the bridge at Tres Puentes, just as Kempt's men did, and walk up onto the knoll of Yruna, where Roman excavations are being carried out. Standing on the knoll gives one an appreciation of the perilous situation in which Kempt could have found himself if the French had turned against him: the spot feels quite isolated. However, looking out to the east from the knoll one can easily picture Brisbane and Colville's brigades bearing down on the bridge of Mendoza, easing the situation and allowing Kempt and the 15th Hussars to advance onto the plain.

83

LEFT **This modernised bridge over the Zadorra in front of Nanclares is the one crossed by Wellington himself, along with Cole's 4th Division and the cavalry of Ponsonby and Robert Hill. Although the bridge has been improved it is still possible to see some of the original buttresses at either end.**

It is very easy and very satisfying to follow Picton's route from the hills to the north of Las Guetas. There are several small tracks which run down from the hills – almost certainly those used by Picton and later by Dalhousie. Once down, Picton debouched onto the plain and headed for Martioda, before advancing on Mendoza and then the bridge over the Zadorra, which lies about half a mile further. Crossing the bridge takes you over to the French-held side of the river, and a turn to the east will bring you first to Margarita and then to La Hermandad (via a bridge over the new motorway). La Hermandad sits on the edge of an industrial estate and has lost some of its aura, although the church still stands and the open ground around it demonstrates why both Colville and Dalhousie had trouble in taking it. Crispiana too has changed somewhat, and stands by a railway line. By turning south from Crispiana you reach Zuazo, a small village which is free from too much development. This was the site of the main French gun position during the afternoon. Falling back towards Vittoria takes you to the village of Ali, and a track from here leads out into what appears to be a protected walking area. A trig point marks the site of the final French position; on the forward slopes Joseph positioned his guns to fire upon the advancing 3rd Division, causing them not inconsiderable casualties.

Behind Ali is the urban sprawl of Vittoria itself. The town has a fine museum with some great dioramas and a good weapons collection. There is a huge memorial to the battle in the Plaza de La Virgen Blanca. Beyond the town lie the villages and roads which were the scene of much of the disorder after the battle. It is easy to imagine the fields to the east of the town choked full of wagons and guns. The village of Zurbano was one of the last to see any action when British light dragoons collided with the rearguard of the Army of Portugal, a fight which is easy to follow. On the whole, the battlefield does much to evoke memories of 1813 in spite of the industrialisation, and with so many bridges and small villages it is easy to pinpoint the positions of the various incidents.

RIGHT **The great memorial to the battle of Vittoria in the Plaza de Virgen Blanca. This massive statue depicts a victorious Wellington receiving the thanks of the locals, while the defeated French troops go skulking off behind. The statue is topped by a lion clutching an eagle in its claws, both of which are crowned by the angel of peace. The memorial also features good statues of Allied infantry and artillerymen. Maybe it would have been pertinent to include some plundering British infantry with their hands 'in the till'.**

OVERLEAF **The storming of San Sebastian, 31 August 1813. This superb painting by Dighton shows Leith's 5th Division during the assault. It was the last time Wellington's army would be called upon to take a town by storm, Pamplona being starved into submission in October the same year. The siege operations on this occasion were supervised by Sir Thomas Graham.**

WARGAMING VITTORIA

INTRODUCTION

Since no one wargame could do justice to both the manoeuvres and the battle described above, I shall, instead, offer various suggestions for portraying different aspects of the Vittoria Campaign in a series of wargames, taking a risk that this approach will in all probability – like Wellington's original plan – fail to succeed completely! The reader must then select whatever combination of games best suits his inclinations and resources.

First, however, some thoughts on the problem of hindsight, which will afflict any participants who, unlike the original generals they will portray in the games, enjoy the great advantage of first having read this account of the campaign. Any wargame which is advertised as 'a recreation of' or 'based upon' Vittoria immediately encourages the players to discover the historical events – if they are not already familiar with them. Such foreknowledge can thwart all the Game Organiser's attempts to create the appropriate mindset before play begins, and must exercise an insidious influence upon decision-making during the game. I would, therefore, suggest that readers consider either the option of writing disguised or fictionalised scenarios and personal briefings to overcome this problem, or make a determined effort to recruit players who have not yet read this book!

'A BRILLIANT STRATEGIC CAMPAIGN': THE MARCH TO VITTORIA

Wellington's strategic plan –an ambitious enveloping manoeuvre by four columns – can best be gamed as a Map Kriegsspiel: each player, relying upon limited information in his personal briefing, intelligence reports and messages from his comrades, together with a subjective picture of the situation on his map, sends written orders and messages to the Umpire, who resolves all manoeuvres and combats on his master map before reporting back only information that would have become known to that player from aides de camp or personal observation.

An interesting variation upon this long-established game structure is Paddy Griffith's Generalship Game, the rules for which may be found in *Napoleonic Wargaming For Fun* (Ward Lock, 1980). In this game each player must also plan his character's personal routine for the forth coming day, deciding how much time to allocate to councils of war, inspecting troops, travelling on horseback or by carriage, personal reconnaissance, writing despatches, eating and sleeping by completing a daily chart, divided into half-hour segments. A player can respond to events and intelligence reports by adjusting his plans for the remainder of the day from the time when he received the information, but may not

alter activities undertaken beforehand. The stylised maps used for this game – simple road nets upon which the distance between adjacent towns or villages represents one day's march – could easily be drawn from the strategic maps in this book, while the corps-level resolution of the original combat system can be adapted quite simply by replacing corps by divisions!

In a game of the manoeuvres before Vittoria, both sides may be played by participants taking the roles of Wellington, his column and divisional commanders, King Joseph Bonaparte, Marshal Jourdan and the army or corps commanders, but the result – especially if the scenario cannot be disguised effectively – will only coincidentally bear much resemblance to the original events. Alternatively, the players may portray the Allied commanders against umpire-controlled French armies that are programmed to respond historically; or they may take the roles of the French officers and have to react to an Allied force programmed to follow Wellington's original orders.

BELOW **The crossing of the river Esla on 31 May 1813. Exhausted British infantry and cavalry climb up onto the riverbank after making the hazardous crossing of the roaring waters of the Esla. Many men were drowned during the passage of the river, many of the infantry being forced to hold on to the stirrups of the cavalry.**

The Game Organiser may prefer to assemble all the participants in one location to play until the opposing armies meet in a climactic battle, fought in one of the ways suggested below, but such a game might also be played day by day, using the telephone or e-mail. Each player would contact the Umpire early in the evening to receive troop locations and states after that day's march, together with any other intelligence or messages that would have arrived during the day. He would then have to draft orders for the following day's march and issue them by contacting the Umpire later that same evening, exactly as would have been done in reality – albeit by aides-de-camp on fast horses, rather than by electronic communication – and would then receive any new information that might have come into headquarters after orders for the day had been sent out, which might necessitate some further orders or messages. The Umpire would then resolve the transmission and arrival of orders, troop manoeuvres on the following day, any contacts with the enemy that did not result in a significant engagement and consequent intelligence reports, ready for the next evening's play. Once the armies concentrate for battle, the Umpire would contact players to arrange a suitable venue and date for the tactical wargame.

BELOW **The bridge over the Zadorra at Tres Puentes. It was here that Kempt's brigade crossed the river unseen by the French before climbing up onto the knoll of Iruna behind. Kempt's men crossed the bridge from right to left as we look, followed shortly afterwards by the 15th Hussars who were sent to support them.**

'A NOTABLE SUCCESS' AND A 'STRANGE SPECTACLE': TACTICAL ENCOUNTERS DURING THE ADVANCE

Two very different engagements which occurred before the concentration at Vittoria suggest themselves as scenarios for low-level tactical games. The cavalry encounter at Morales de Toro could be fought using any conventional wargame rules, or players could portray individual officers in the Hussar regiments concerned and 'experience' the charge in a similar roleplay to those I have described in the wargaming appendices to Campaign Series Numbers 6, *Balaclava 1854*, and 7, *Alexander 334-323BC*. The combat at San Millan offers a battle between two infantry divisions that provides a most unusual scenario for a traditional tabletop engagement, that will challenge both the players and whatever set of rules is employed! Many of the alternative ideas for controlling games of the individual columns, described below, would be equally applicable to this encounter.

THE BATTLE OF VITTORIA

WHOLE BATTLE GAMES

One option would be to have a large floor model of the Vittoria battle-field, across which a team of Umpires would move bodies of troops in accordance with the players' orders, either ticked off on a 'menu' of tactical commands upon a form completed each turn, or displayed on easily read flashcards from their seats around the hall. Such a game structure can accommodate a large number of players, so that every division, or even brigade, has a different commander, creating the possibility that orders may go astray, be misinterpreted or even disobeyed – all of which occurred in the historical engagement. A detailed description of this type game may be found in Campaign Series Number 48, *Salamanca 1812.* If insufficient participants can be mustered to command both sides, there is no reason why the majority of those taking part should not command the French armies against a few players giving orders to selected Allied formations, the remaining Allied forces being umpire-controlled or programmed to follow their original orders and/or actions.

In such a case, I would recommend the Allied players take the roles of officers in General Lord Dalhousie's Left Centre Column, and that the game commence with Sir Thomas Picton's decision to attack. If there are enough Allied players to command two columns, the Game Organiser can choose whether to appoint them to General Cole's Right Centre Column and concentrate upon the fighting against Gazan's Army of the South, or to portray the attempt of General Graham's Left Column to cut the French line of retreat along the high road to Bayonne. The operations of General Hill's Right Column in the heights of Puebla can be assumed to follow their historical course and omitted, or information as to his progress generated by dice, taking into account any fresh French troops despatched to that sector of the battlefield, as it would prove extremely difficult to recreate the terrain convincingly upon the tabletop.

To wargame the battle at home, with only a few players, the Game Organiser could use 1/300 scale troops upon a much smaller terrain model and the Army-level rules from *Napoleonic Wargaming For Fun*, or Kriegsspiel troop-blocks upon a map together with the original von Reisswitz rules of 1824, translated and published by Bill Leeson.

Such a game might concentrate, on the Allied side, upon either Wellington's original perspective from the knoll above Nanclares or, later, from the hill behind Villodas, or that of one of his column commanders, the other columns being umpire-controlled, according to the player's pre-battle instructions or Wellington's historical orders. The player can send orders and messages, but will only receive intelligence gradually, according to his position on the battlefield. The French might be commanded by one or two players, portraying Joseph and Jourdan, or might have separate commanders for each army.

SIMULTANEOUS BATTLE GAMES

Another way to tackle Vittoria would be to set up separate tables and games for each area of the battlefield – the tables, perhaps, arranged in a different, ahistorical, orientation to prevent players having an unrealistically clear overview of the battle. Again, the operations of Hill's and/or Graham's columns might be omitted. The various times at which troops first became engaged in different areas could be used to allow redeployment of players 'killed', 'gravely wounded' or 'captured' in other areas, or of Allied commanders too badly defeated to make further progress into other columns.

INDIVIDUAL COLUMN/INCIDENT GAMES

Rather than attempt to refight the entire battle of Vittoria, the Game Organiser may prefer to concentrate, for example, upon the experiences of General Graham's column, strangely omitted altogether from the wargame recreation proposed by Lieutenant-Colonel J.P. Lawford in *Vitoria 1813*, the relevant volume in the *Knight's Battles for Wargamers* series. It was, indeed, a separate engagement from the main battle, but as a wargame offers an obvious chance to change history if the British commander will be bolder; equally the French might keep open the high road to Bayonne and reduce the consequences of defeat – assuming that events elsewhere on the battlefield follow their historical course – for the rest of army.

The fighting around Aranguiz, Abechuco, Gamarra Mayor, Gamarra Minor and Durana forms an ideal subject for a disguised scenario. The Game Organiser can quite easily deceive prospective players by simply changing the orientation of the map, so that the attackers are advancing from the east or south-east, and altering the place names. He can also reverse the nationalities of the combatants, or – still keeping a Peninsular War background – have French forces opposing Spaniards in 1808. Alternatively, the action could be set in another theatre of the Napoleonic Wars, or even in another early nineteenth-century campaign, fought with similar weapon technology, such as the United States' War with Mexico in 1847.

Another option would be to play a detailed brigade or battalion level game centred upon one incident, such as the crossing of the Zadorra at Yruna by Kempt's Brigade of the Light Division; Sir Thomas Picton's attack at Mendoza – an ideal subject for wargamers who prefer initiative to obeying orders! – or to follow Brigade-Major Harry Smith's account of his part, quoted at length in a footnote in Oman's *History*, in directing Vandeleur's Brigade of the Light Division to take the village of La Hermandad.

Players would take the roles of battalion, squadron and battery commanders, staff officers and aides-de-camp. This game would attempt to portray the detail of the drill and tactics of the period, and hence the time taken to change formation or facing – something factored out of division level wargame rules, where the countermarching necessary to face about is omitted and the unit simply reversed – by demanding that players display flashcards of the contemporary words of command, in the correct sequence, to give orders to their troops.

ABOVE **Wellington, telescope in hand, watches as British infantry advance during the battle of Vittoria.**

For contemporary tactics, readers are recommended to consult *Imperial Bayonets: Tactics of the Napoleonic Battery, Battalion and Brigade as found in Contemporary Regulations* by George Nafziger (Greenhill Books, 1995); and for greater detail of Sir David Dundas's Principles of Military Movements &c, including words of command, a facsimile of *The Eighteen Manoeuvres, as practised by His Majesty's Infantry* by Serjeant Thomas Langley, of the 1st Royal Regiment Tower Hamlets Militia, 1794, an epitome, with explanatory diagrams – and thus ideal for wargamers – published by Bill Leeson. From latter publisher may also be obtained a facsimile copy of *Memorandums of Field Exercise for the Troops of Gentlemen and Yeomen Cavalry by An Officer of Light Dragoons*, 1795, which will be especially useful should one wish to recreate the cavalry action at Morales de Toro. For the French drill and tactics of the same period, see *Tactics and Grand Tactics of the Napoleonic Wars* by George Jeffrey. With a practised team of umpires moving the figures or company troop blocks on a large model terrain, such a game should be able to proceed in real time.

A GUIDE TO FURTHER READING

Surprisingly, given its great importance, no single volume has ever been written in English on the Vittoria campaign of 1813. Instead historians have chosen to include it in general studies of the war. The five main sources for the study of the campaign – indeed, any Peninsular War campaign – are Wellington's own *Dispatches and Supplementary Dispatches* and the works of Napier, Oman and Fortescue. Within the pages of these multi-volume works can be found all the background detail to Wellington and his Peninsular campaign. Of course, there are other specialist studies which are of great use when branching off into other areas, but these five works are simply indispensable. It is possible to follow the often-complicated lead-up to the Vittoria campaign from start to finish in *Dispatches*, while both Oman and Fortescue provide in-depth accounts of the campaign and include the vital strengths of both armies at the outset of the campaign. Fortescue loaned the French statistics to Oman for the latter's monumental work, and we should be grateful for such co-operation between two great historians of the age.

The tactics, uniforms and weapons used in the Peninsula are the subject of scores of books; among the best are Osprey's Men-at-Arms, Elite and Warrior series. An exhaustive study of the battle from the French side can be found in Sarramon's *La Bataille de Vittoria*, which gives useful maps illustrating the various stages of the battle.

Eye-witness accounts of the war will always be a prime source of material, and the Peninsular War spawned many fine accounts – too many to be listed here, although I have listed the major biographies of both Hill and Graham. There are good bibliographies in Oman's *Wellington's Army*, Brett James' *Life in Wellington's Army* and in Sutcliffe's *Sandler Collection*. The latter is most helpful and, although by no means complete, benefits from the editor's own comments.

Delavoye, A.M., *Life of Thomas Graham, Lord Lynedoch* (London 1880)

Fletcher, I., *Wellington's Regiments* (London 1995)

Fortescue, Sir John, *History of the British Army* (London 1899-1930)

Gurwood, J. (Ed.), *Dispatches of Field Marshal the Duke of Wellington* (London 1837-39)

Haythornthwaite, P.J., *Weapons and Equipment of the Napoleonic Wars* (1979)

Napier, Sir William, *A History of the War in the Peninsula and the South of France*

Oman, Sir Charles, *History of the Peninsular War*, Vol. VI (Oxford 1922)

Sarramon, J., *La Bataille de Vittoria* (Paris 1985)

Sidney, Rev. E., *Life of Lord Hill* (London 1845)

Wellington, *Supplementary Dispatches and Memoranda* (London 1857-72)

Windrow, M. & Embleton, G., *Military Dress of the Peninsular War* (London 1974)

INDEX

Figures in **bold** refer to illustrations

Alava, General Miguel de (1771-1843) **26**
Albuera, battle of, 16th May 1811 11
Ali **68**
Allied forces *see also* British forces
  failure to pursue the French 73, 75
  French army routs 69
  Longa's Division 46, 48, 61-62, 63
  Morillo's Division 40-41
  order of battle **30-31**(table)
  Peninsular War 6
  at Vittoria 59, 60-61, 64-65
  the pursuit 71, 73
Arinez 56-57, **57**
Arinez, knoll of 35, **44**, **52**, 53, 81-82
Arriaga 68
artillery, the great duel **58-59**, 59, 60,
  60
Austria 76

Badajoz, siege of 11-12, 12
Bayonne 77
Bayonne road 35, 46, 61, 63
Betono 68
Bonaparte, Joseph, King of Spain
  (1768-1844) 8, **28**, 29, 36
  confidence 39
  flight of 72, **72**, **76**
  orders retreat 68
  recalled to France 75
  views of battlefield **36**
Bonaparte, Napoleon (1769-1821) 6,
  20
  abdication 78
  and Spanish throne 7
British forces **8-9**, 14, 17-18 *see also*
  Allied forces
  1st (Howard's) Division 62-63, 70
  2nd (Hill's) Division 21-22, 22
    at Vittoria 40-41, **41**, 54-56
  3rd (Picton's) Division 49, 56, 56-57,
    69
    storms Mendoza bridge 52, **54-55**
  5th (Oswald's) Division 68, 70
    in action at Gamarra Major 45-46,
    46-47, 48, **48**, 61
  7th (Dalhousie's) Division 49, 57-58
  Light Division 48, 49, 56, 58
    at San Millan 24
  artillery **58-59**, 59
  cavalry 23, **64-65**, 70, 72, **72**, 72-73
  crosses the Esla river 22, **89**
  dispatched to Portugal **6**, 8
  at Vittoria **65**, 69-70
Burgos, siege of 14, 17, 23

casualties

Badajoz 12
  San Millan 24
  Vittoria 73
chronology **16**(table)
Cintra, Convention of 8
Ciudad Rodrigo 12, 14, 21
Clausel, Bertrand (1772-1842) 24, 39,
  75
convoy, the 24, 71, 73
Corunna, battle of, 16th January 1809
  8-9, 10

Dalhousie, Lieutenant General Sir
  George Ramsay, Earl (1770-1838)
  27, 38, 49, 58
Dickson, Colonel Alexander (1777-
  1840) 59
dispositions **42-43**(map), **50-51**(map),
  66-67(map)
  Allied 37-39, 60
  French 20, 36-37, 60, **61**, **69**
Douro river **9**, 22
Durana 45, 46, 48, 61-62, 63, 68
  bridge 56, **74-75**

Ebro river **10**, **12**, 23, 24
Elvina **8-9**
Erlon, General Jean-Baptiste, Count d'
  (1765-1844) 29, **29**, 61, 65
Esla river **20-21**, 22, **89**

Foy, General Maximilien Sebastien,
  comte (1775-1825) 20, 75
French forces 20, 22, 23
  Army of Portugal 36-37, 45, 68
  Army of the Centre 36, 68
  Army of the North 39
  Army of the South 36, 68, 70-71
  artillery 59
  cavalry 36
  invasion of Portugal 10, 10-11
  invasion of Spain 6
  loots convoy 73
  morale 76-77
  at Nivelle 77
  order of battle **32-33**(table)
  remnants 75
  at San Millan 24
  Spanish troops 46, 48
  at Vittoria 44, 53, 56, 61
    defends Arinez 57
    defends bridge at Mendoza 52
    defends Gamarra Major 48, **49**
    defends heights of Puebla 40-41,
    54, 55-56
    defends La Hermandad 57, 58
    redeploys 53-54, 58-59

withdrawal 69, **69**

Gamarra Mayor 45, **46-47**, **48**, 61
  bridge at 48, **48-49**, 64
  French withdrawal 68
Gamarra Minor 45
Gazan, Countess 73
Gazan, General Honore Theodore
  Maxime (1765-1845) 29, 64-65, 71
Graham, General Sir Thomas (1748-
  1843) 22, **27**, 27-28
  at Vittoria 38-39, 45, 48, 62
  engages Foy 75
Great Britain 6, 8
guerrillas 20

Hill, Sir Rowland (1772-1842) 26-27,
  35, 37

intelligence 20, 24

Jourdan, Marshal Jean Baptiste, Count
  (1762-1833) **29**, 39
  errors 44
  experience 29
  recalled to France 75
  at Vittoria 44, 53-54
Junot, General Jean Andoche, duc
  d'Abrantes (1771-1813) 6-7, 8

La Hermandad 35, 57-58, **80**, 84
lines of communication 23
  French 39, 46, 63
Longa, General Francisco (1770-1831)
  27, 28
looting 73, **78-79**

Margarita 56
Massena, Marshal André (1758-1817)
  10-11
memorials 84, **85**
Mendoza, bridge at 52, **54-55**, **81**, 83,
  84
Moore, Lieutenant General Sir John
  (1761-1809) 8, 10
Morales de Toro, action at, 2nd June
  1813 **8**, 23
Morillo, General Pablo **27**, 28
Murray, George, Quartermaster
  General 18

Nivelle, battle of, 10th November 1813
  77

Orthes, battle of, 27th February 1814
  78
Ortiz de Zarate, Jose 49

Pamplona 77
Peninsular War, the 6-8, **7**(map), 10-12, 13
Picton, Lieutenant General Sir Thomas (1758-1815) **26**, 84
experience 27
at Vittoria 38, 53, 56
bridge at Mendoza 52, **54-55**
Portugal, French conquest 6-7
prisoners 22, **94**
Puebla, heights of 35, **56**, **60**, 82
assault on 40-41, **41**, 44, 54-56, **62-63**
Puebla de Arganzon, bridge **34**
Puente Arenas, bridge **10**

Reille, General Honore Charles Michel Joseph, Comte de (1775-1860) **28**
experience 29
at Vittoria 45, 68, 69-70

Salamanca 21-22
battle of, 22nd July 1812 14
Salvatierra road 70, 71, **71**
San Martin de Lines **12**
San Millan **12-13**, **13**, 81
action at, 18th June 1813 **22**(map), 24

San Sebastian 77, **86-87**
Soult, Marshal Nicolas Jean de Dieu (1769-1851) 10, 11, 20
takes command 75-76, 76-77, 77-78
Spain 7-8, 8
Subjiana de Alava **40**, 41, 44, 53
Subjiana de Morillos **23**

Talavera, battle of, 27th-28th July 1809 10
terrain, Vittoria 35-36, **39**, **82-83**
theatre of operations **18-19**(map), **38**(map), **74**(map)
Toulouse, battle of, 10th April 1814 78
Tres Puentes 35
bridge at **45**, 49, 83, **90**

Villa Velha, camp at **10-11**
Villodas, bridge at **44**, 48-49
Vittoria 35-36, 81, 84
battle of **17**, **61**
consequences of 76

Wargaming 88-93
Wellington, Arthur Wellesly, 1st Duke of (1769-1852) 22, 23, **25**, **26**, **77**

appointed Commander in Chief of the Spanish Army 18
artillery 59
attempts to intercept Clausel 75
enters France 77
experience 25-26
military chest 73
and Picton 27
plans 20-21, 37
on plundering 73
in Portugal 6, 9, 10-11, 12, **14-15**
'provisional' battalions 17-18
reconnaissance 35
reputation 14
retreats to Ciudad Rodrigo 14
secures Salamanca 21-22
senior officers 18
and Soult 76, 77-78
strategic advantages 23-24
at Vittoria **37**, 45, **53**, **57**, **70**, **92-93**
deploys for final attack 60
view **34**
at Villodas 48-49

Zadorra river 35, **45**, **82-83**, **84**
Zurbano 69, 70, **70**, 84

COMPANION SERIES FROM OSPREY

MEN-AT-ARMS

An unrivalled source of information on the organisation, uniforms and equipment of the world's fighting men, past and present. The series covers hundreds of subjects spanning 5,000 years of history. Each 48-page book includes concise texts packed with specific information, some 40 photos, maps and diagrams, and eight colour plates of uniformed figures.

ELITE

Detailed information on the uniforms and insignia of the world's most famous military forces. Each 64-page book contains some 50 photographs and diagrams, and 12 pages of full-colour artwork.

NEW VANGUARD

Comprehensive histories of the design, development and operational use of the world's armoured vehicles and artillery. Each 48-page book contains eight pages of full-colour artwork including a detailed cutaway.

WARRIOR

Definitive analysis of the armour, weapons, tactics and motivation of the fighting men of history. Each 64-page book contains cutaways and exploded artwork of the warrior's weapons and armour.

ORDER OF BATTLE

The most detailed information ever published on the units which fought history's great battles. Each 96-page book contains comprehensive organisation diagrams supported by ultra-detailed colour maps. Each title also includes a large fold-out base map.

AIRCRAFT OF THE ACES

Focuses exclusively on the elite pilots of major air campaigns, and includes unique interviews with surviving aces sourced specifically or each volume. Each 96-page volume contains up to 40 specially commissioned artworks, unit listings, new scale plans and the best archival photography available.

COMBAT AIRCRAFT

Technical information from the world's leading aviation writers on the aircraft types flown. Each 96-page volume contains up to 40 specially commissioned artworks, unit listings, new scale plans and the best archival photography available.